W9-APN-562

POETRY AND FAITH

by the same author

GUIDE TO CARLYLE

CRITIQUES

A HISTORY OF SHAKESPEARIAN CRITICISM

LATER CRITIQUES

AUGUSTUS RALLI

POETRY AND FAITH

THE BODLEY HEAD : LONDON

First published 1951

Printed and bound in Great Britain by
WILLIAM CLOWES AND SONS, LIMITED, LONDON AND BECCLES
for JOHN LANE THE BODLEY HEAD LTD.
8, Bury Place, London, W.C.1

CONTENTS

PREFACE

Should the question be asked why such old subjects as Homer, Virgil, etc., have been selected for further criticism in the title essay, the explanation is, as a protest against the tendency of much modern literary criticism to become almost scientific, and to be written for the specialist rather than the cultured layman. I was confirmed in my choice by an article of George Sampson's—*Literature in the Class-Room* (Essays and Studies by Members of the English Association, Vol. 20)—in which he deplores the danger to the student of a class-room course in literature that sets him up for life with third-hand and fourth-hand generalities, instead of urging him to wrestle in solitude with a great work of creative art and say, 'I will not let thee go except thou bless me'. This agrees with Brunetière's saying, that in every great work of art or literature there is something hidden which is only revealed to sympathy.

IMAGINATION AND REALITY

IMAGINATION AND REALITY

The spiritual and economic troubles from which the world is suffering react upon each other. Anxiety for self-preservation depresses the spirit, and the depressed spirit magnifies the importance of material things. The scene where modern life is lived has been appropriately called the 'world-city', from which leisure, silence, solitude, romance are excluded, where there is no time for disinterested admiration of a higher soul, where money is the grand regulator in human relations. Telephones, motors, aeroplanes, wireless, machines of all kinds have annihilated distance, and man is face to face with man as never before. The result is that in 1938 persons of authority declared Europe to be in a more savage condition than for the last thousand years.

The soul needs solitude and leisure in which to grow, and both are impossible under modern conditions. The shadow of the world-city falls on the remotest country districts, and the labourer in the fields has become town-minded. Leisure may be the portion of the rich, but the different classes are now so economically united that the minds of the rich are ill at ease. To live on investment income and spend one's days reading the best literature in the world sounds an ideal existence, were it not for this economic unity. The minds of the fortunate few are distracted by the thought of the over-driven professional man, the workers in office and shop, in mine and factory, the inhabitants of slum and tenement—of the long hours of labour and scanty rest of those whose arch-terror is that they may lose even this work which is all that enables them to maintain their hold on life. The man who needs not earn his own living has missed a great opportunity, and feels himself cut off from those who do, and at a disadvantage with them.

And yet this was not so in the past. The English aristocracy of the eighteenth century was the most privileged class that has ever existed, and its members had no doubts about their position. Edward FitzGerald affirmed England's greatest product to be her country gentlemen: the distinguishing glory of England, in his opinion, as the arts were of Greece, or war of Rome. Man is not to be saved by work alone, and the effect of work upon the character is evil as well as good. There are certain virtues that can only be acquired through leisure and independence of material cares, and it is an old saying that education takes three generations to fulfil itself. The essence of work is competition, and competition implies hostility to one's fellow creatures. The worker is at war with his neighbours; he must overthrow them in order to rise, and make his profits by their losses. Hence it is his duty to study their faults rather than their virtues, and the resulting habit of mind is not a noble one. It leads him to a low view of human nature, to disbelief in the possibility of a generous action, and to regard self-interest as the universal motive of humanity. It makes him cynical, suspicious, and unfriendly, and narrows his affections to those whose interests are identical with his own. The new-rich is usually a man of outstanding ability, yet he is universally disliked, and there is always a reason for age-long prejudices.

The essence of work being competition, it follows that the worker assumes all men to be born enemies, and it is needless to say that this is the opposite pole to education and civilization. However impracticable, the wish is present in the depth of every human heart to see the reign of love and the Kingdom of God established on earth. And the fact that in simpler ages it was possible to live a life of leisure without self-reproach, and the man of leisure was honoured by the worker for the very reason that he was exempted from competition, proves that there are certain virtues which need such protection to develop. The nobleman of former days was looked upon as the exemplar of a higher life, and this was an ideal for those below him—an objective which all alike desired to attain. May we not say that England has a fascination for other countries, and that even the abuse which a certain kind of foreigner lavishes upon England is proof of this fascination? The reason is that class distinctions are still softened by feudal memories—when Gurth the thrall of Cedric bore witness by his brass collar that he belonged to the family of Cedric—and that differences due to birth do not cause the bitterness between men as do those which spring from competition for means of living, or place, or power. Over the England of the early eighteenth century, consisting of aristocracy, gentry, professional classes, and peasantry, the 'black pox of Industry'—as Don S. de Madariaga calls it—has broken out and never ceased to extend its ravages[1]; but if, among unspoilt surroundings, a few large estates have even now survived the death duties, there will be found something of the old tradition which gave to English country life a portion of the divine realized on earth.

However, we must face the dilemma that nowadays all men must work or pay the price in loss of self-respect and pangs of conscience, but that work and competition exclude those virtues which in the past made one class the symbol of a higher order of being. The late Lord Middleton, in his *Memoirs*, preserved a saying of Lady Airlie's, in reply to his suggestion that the next generation, whether landed or not, would have learned to work: 'You forget; a gentleman lives on what he has; he does not work.'[2] A certain great nobleman of the nineteenth century said of his brother,

[1] *Anarchy or Hierarchy*, pp. 207–8.
[2] *The Times*, March 2, 1939.

a distinguished scientist, 'He is not a gentleman, he works'; and this, though an overstatement, had the grain of truth that there are certain virtues which can only be acquired by the third generation of those who have lived free from care. It may be due to the decline of country life that the outlook for the future is the reverse of promising. Scott was more solicitous to be a country gentleman than an author—to his ultimate ruin. In days not so far distant, if a man made a fortune he bought an estate and attempted to found a county family. As the generations succeeded, the kindly earth drew from his descendants their savage characteristics and substituted the peace of nature, and gave them gracious manners. In these days the half-educated inheritors of new-made wealth are cast upon the ocean of the town, with no opportunity to acquire old traditions, and every opportunity to take their fill of coarse animal pleasures. And the forceful personalities and opinions, also bequeathed to them by the original money-maker, prevent the humble-mindedness needed to acquire true knowledge.

To this dilemma of work and inherited leisure the first answer is that these theories about work imply the reality of earthly life. Philosophers tell us that all serious thought begins with a meditation on death. The modern errors of the totalitarian State, or the totalitarian family of some continental nations, spring from a like false thought—that man is a native of this earth instead of an exile from the land of the spirit. The moral law cannot be located in our midst but comes from beyond the boundaries of human institutions. Communists call religion the opium of the people because it is the greatest obstacle to their schemes; and there is a French epigram that a good father of a family is capable of anything. But no sooner are bodily needs supplied than the voice of the spirit is heard. The higher does Fortune heap her material favours, the deeper is the void of the soul. Man is on this earth for a purpose, but not to make a home of it and take his ease. Plotinus explained religious experience as the finding of his true home by the exile. 'Our hearts find no rest until we rest in Thee' is the famous prayer of St. Augustine.

The earth is best described as the vale of soul-making, and it is in reasoning back from this position that we get the true value of material things. If we accept the statement that the human soul is part of the universal soul, confined in the body that it may acquire individuality from its struggle with matter, it follows that we reject all philosophies of asceticism that condemn matter as an evil thing. If earthly life has its part to play in the development of the soul, matter can be equally noble as base. It is the function of art so to use the beauty of earth as to make it a symbol of heaven. The mystic dares the final bound and actually leaves his body to explore super-material regions; the poet is concerned with that shining borderland where the two worlds intermingle. What gives him the right to be our guide in these things is that faculty of imagination which has been called semi-divine. 'Style is the body of literature', said Saintsbury, 'but imagination the soul.' The value of every work of art is according to the amount of imagination which it contains, but as the word has often been ill-defined and has not yet freed itself from some erroneous associations, it is necessary to re-define it, to make clear our way.

In popular speech imagination is identified either with the inventive power of the mind or its picture-making power. To the first, the inventive, is due the tendency to regard imagination as a luxury-faculty—unreal, unsubstantial, divorced from practical life.[1] Rather it is the power to place a thing in its relation to the universe, and therefore the truths which it brings home are more real than any direct transcript

[1] Émile Legouis quotes the saying of Pascal that imagination is the 'teacher of untruth', and that of Malebranche, that it is the 'mad inmate of the mind' (*Early Life of Wordsworth*, p. 418).

from so-called reality.[1] When Thucydides describes the sufferings of the Greek army in its retreat from Syracuse, and the wholesale slaughter at the Assinarus river, we think less of the physical horrors—though these are salient enough—than of the great mind of the writer as he mediates between the soul of the world and poor mortal man. Far otherwise is it when, in a modern book on Robespierre, we read of processions to the guillotine and a scaffold slippery with blood. However, we will force a writer to bear witness against himself. Rousseau conceived the *Nouvelle Héloïse* as an escape from reality; he was so disgusted with life that he sought refuge in the 'land of chimaeras', as he called it; it seemed to him that no true love or friendship was left on earth, so he would create them out of pure mind. But this fairy gold has become withered leaves to our modern world, not to be compared for beauty and reality with his account of his love for the Comtesse d'Houdetot—a page taken from his own book of life: and so we conclude that reality best deserves its name when touched by imagination.

To see a thing in its relation to the universal is the ideal, but there are degrees of fulfilment according to the progress

[1] A. C. Bradley distinguishes between the limited knowledge of science and the universal knowledge to which poetry, by means of imagination, comes nearest: '. . . these literally true ideas are, in another and fuller sense, the least true of ideas; for the most true idea of the object would be that of these objects in their relation to everything else in the universe. In other words, a perfectly true idea of any one thing would include a perfectly true idea of everything else. That means again, it would be the true idea of the whole or the infinite, and that would be the only true idea'; '. . . if you try to say that anything short of it (the whole) is ultimately real you are considering a part in abstraction from the rest, and then it would be inconsistent. It will be pretending to stand alone and be complete, although you know that it has relations to something beyond it' (*Ideals of Religion*, pp. 210, 222). Cf. W. G. de Burgh, '. . . every object of thought is so linked with every other object, that none is what it is in utter isolation . . . in each there is in some sense involved the structure of the whole world' (*Towards a Religious Philosophy*, p. 82).

of the writer's mind, and it is from such stages that we learn about imagination. In the opening pages of the *French Revolution* Carlyle describes the decline of kingship throughout France, and how, when Louis XV lay sick unto death, his name was hardly mentioned: 'hardly', he says, 'in the immeasurable tide of French speech which ceases not day after day and only ebbs towards the short hours of night'. This is one of its author's purest imaginative effects, belonging to his best period, and is to be contrasted with some of his more romantic and more gorgeous effects: for, much as he would have disdained the name, Carlyle was a romantic. Many critics have discussed romanticism, but none more ably than Mr. F. L. Lucas. He sees it as 'the expression of the imagination and the emotions unchecked by a sense of reality and a sense of society'; and he calls the Middle Ages the romantic's spiritual home, his desire being for something distant, for 'la princesse lointaine'. We will reinforce this with Carlyle's saying that the past seems beautiful because the haggard element of fear is withdrawn from it, and we will turn to his description of the parting with his family of Louis XVI on the eve of his execution—surely the most poignant parting scene ever written: 'The sorrows we gave each other; the poor joys we faithfully shared, and all our lovings and our sufferings, and confused toilings under the earthly Sun are over.' We will shortly return to this, merely remarking now that its beauty is more of earth than heaven.

Coleridge affirmed that imagination gives unity to variety and sees all things in one; and he quotes from Jeremy Taylor, that 'he who seeth all things in one may enjoy true peace and rest of spirit'. 'The primary Imagination', says Coleridge, 'I hold to be the living power and prime agent of all human perception, and as a repetition in the finite mind of the eternal act of creation in the infinite I AM.'[1] May we not then say that the imaginative part of art is the soul's

[1] *Biographia Literaria*, Chapters IV, XII, XIII.

contribution—its effort to place everything in its relation to the universal? If this world is the vale of soul-making, and the soul, which is part of the universal, is confined in matter so that it may acquire separate identity, it attempts to reveal to the intellect its true nature, it speaks to the intellect from within its prison walls the language of the universal, and according as the intellect interprets these messages are they rightly or wrongly delivered to the world. The imagination originates in heaven and stoops to earth; the intellect arises from earth and aspires to heaven. The intellect has been slowly evolving in man ever since he emerged from the brute, making sure of its conquests one by one, and methodically extending its dominion over nature. The schoolmen once believed in a science of sciences, such as logic, which might lead to universal knowledge. The career of the world's greatest all-round genius, Leonardo da Vinci, rather supports this theory of a single method. He meditated submarine boats and diving apparatus, poison gas, armoured cars, propulsion by steam, wireless telegraphy, and aeroplanes. In astronomy he anticipated Galileo and Newton, in anatomy Harvey, in mathematics Einstein.[1] The intellect, therefore, is slowly reclaiming the world-jungle; the imagination, an originally perfect faculty, is hindered from full working by the imperfect human brain.

On this subject we can learn much from the later romantics—those who belong to the romantic revival, as it is called—such as Carlyle and the Brontës, especially Charlotte, for the soul of Emily was often strong enough to soar above the clouds. They cannot forget the earth, and are haunted by that fear the absence of which, in Carlyle's words, makes the past beautiful; and this confirms the saying of Mr. Lucas—that the romantic always yearns for what is far off. The cause of his fear is simply man—the populations of the towns that arose with the Industrial Revolution and from scattered blots on the surface of nature now threaten to

[1] *The Times*, March 31, 1938.

shadow the entire globe. To many of us there is something melancholy in a great city, a succession of streets with tall buildings that shut out the sky—and when we walk through unfamiliar streets we are subject to a peculiar kind of depression. For when man is excluded from nature he loses his religion and traditions, becomes utterly matter-of-fact, jealous of his fellows, nerve-ridden, combative, and efficient in material things rather than spiritual.[1] 'The aspect of that man jarred the music of my soul for the rest of the day', said Carlyle of a certain unsympathetic literary person; and when he visited the model prisons he recoiled from the 'ape faces' and 'angry dog faces' of their inmates. Dr. Johnson preferred Fleet Street to natural beauty, and, driving in a post-chaise, compared the open country with annihilation, and arrival at a town with return to life: but he suffered all his life from hypochondria. Had he sought out Nature, who, one great writer says, 'is never sought in vain', and another that 'she never betrays the heart that loves her', he might have found relief from his agony of mind.

However beautiful, therefore, Carlyle's parting scene is on the lower imaginative level because, through fear, the world is too much with him. Death appears more terrible because it is inflicted by the members of a revolutionary mob whose passions have long festered in mean streets and maddened one another. It is like the sunset that owes its beauty to earth, to the particles of dust that hang in the air and are the cause of the splendid colours. Is not the very idea of parting a kind of St. Peter's denial? The soul is universal and omnipresent, independent of time and space, and knows nothing of parting: but here the dust and tumult of earth have blotted out the eternal stars. When romanticism arises in an old world it can only flourish at the cost of great suffering to the romantic artist on the occasions when he meets

[1] 'Vulgarity is not natural coarseness, but conventional coarseness learned from others' (Hazlitt).

reality; and though the result may be an additional beauty—a strange compound of earth and heaven—there is more of earth than heaven, and so the repose of the highest art is lacking. When Dante would speak with the lovers who are buffeted eternally by the winds of the Inferno, Francesca answers that she will speak and listen, if only they may have respite from the storm:

'Mentre chè il vento, come fa, ci tace'.[1]

A similar yearning note sounds in the voice of the modern romantic—as of one who speaks in the brief interval between a storm that has just died away and another about to begin. A strong soul like Emily Brontë can overcome fear, but I will illustrate the point from a passage in Balzac—the decline and death of old Madame Grandet. Harassed by her miser husband, this woman's whole life had been one long struggle against petty household cares. Day by day she had to account for every ounce of sugar, butter, flour, well knowing that to exceed the limit would provoke storms of rage. People's habits stamp them, and she withered under this persecution. But at the approach of death the burden was lifted; all the bourgeois coarseness vanished from her face; she became beautiful. The preparation for earthly dismissal left the soul free to inhabit its own. Carlyle's parting shakes our faith in the moral order of the universe ; Balzac restores it through the native beauty of the human form. We must guard against the romantic who, by casting longing glances back to earth, hinders the soul's attempts to interpret the universal and charms our ears with the song of the sirens.

The late-born romantic has found his soul but cannot extricate it from the bog of man-made traditions of the immediate past, from the time the world became industrialized and commercialized. His acquired knowledge conflicts with his inheritance, and he suffers the pains of the

[1] 'While the wind, as now, is silent.'

spiritually half-developed who apply infinite faculties to finite things. He worships the creature rather than the Creator and is disappointed because people are ungrateful. The inner voice tells him that he is immortal, but he doubts it when he looks out upon the world, and he shudders at the flight of time that bears him toward the grave and will separate him from the friends too well beloved. Such a being reminds us of the virtuous pagans whom Dante met in the outer circles of the Inferno, with their look of authority, their slow, grave eyes, and sweet voices. To the soul, past and present are an illusion; its only time is the eternal Now. The aesthetic equivalent is the waking trance to which poetry subdues us, and to which rhyme contributes by repeating like sounds. But the eternal Now affects the poet for ill in his earthly relations. It makes the whole of his life constantly present to him, and the sufferings of childhood poignant in old age.[1] We think of Milton's violent political hatreds; of the letters written by Dante to the Florentines that made his recall from exile impossible. Poets of different periods and quality witness how those who do not experience time as succession can be affected. Nothing could assuage Swift's regret for his departed political triumphs; or that of Burns for his brilliant passage across the Edinburgh social world. Rousseau's life was a nightmare of remorse, fear of persecution, unsatisfied craving for revenge. Pope and Voltaire brooded for years over scratches from the meanest enemies, that would not heal. Dr. Johnson was ever haunted by memories of his early poverty and homelessness in London. The convulsive starts which escaped him in solitude were caused by the sting of some unbearable memory, some action of the past which he regretted; and for this reason he dreaded solitude. Charlotte Brontë was likewise haunted by the sufferings of herself and her sisters at

1 'To these qualities he (the poet) has added a disposition to be affected more than other men by absent things as if they were present' (Wordsworth, *Preface*).

the charity school. After fifty years Trollope still felt the 'burn' of his schoolboy sorrows. Lafcadio Hearn confessed that only hard work could divert his mind from vexation and anger and imaginings and recollections of unpleasant things said or done. It is true that there are compensations to the poet, when the sun of a happy time in the past re-arises in memory. Over a visit to an old scene, a meeting with an old friend, is shed a light from beyond. The eternal Now is restored, and the horror of time as succession forgotten. But most poets reveal the painful struggle of souls which have become spirit enough to recognize time as eternal present, yet are still landlocked in the region where time is succession, because, due to their exquisite nerves, they have loved to excess their fellow men, and all earthly beauty of form and colour and music. They suffer mortal pains with immortal powers. Emily Brontë tells how Catherine Linton dreamt that she died and went to heaven, but was homesick for her native moors, until the angels cast her back upon earth, and she awoke sobbing with joy.

Imagination is concerned with earth only so far as it can use it for symbols of beauty. The sacred way of the mystics is closed to most mortals because language has no means of conveying supersensuous experience.[1] Imagination offers an open road, because ninety-nine persons out of a hundred are capable of understanding great literature—if only they make the right approach—by small beginnings, and few books, and persistent returns after intervals to the same book. For it is the truth that literature has a purpose other than its own immediate one: though this has been fiercely contradicted at many periods, and notably in the last decade of the nineteenth century. It can convey moral-aesthetic truth of such a kind as to influence our daily life in more practical fashion than any scientific, historic, or even economic treatise.

[1] 'The technique of meditation is probably about as difficult as the technique of violin-playing' (Aldous Huxley, *Ends and Means*, p. 289).

Stevenson said that if Shakespeare had been knocked on the head in one of his early poaching expeditions, the world would have wagged on very much as it has done, and no one would have known the loss. I do not think this is true, and Stevenson would be the last writer to resent difference of opinion. However heretical it sounds to assign a utilitarian office to poetry, I believe it is the supreme educative influence of our lives.

To deny that life is affected by reading is to give literature a very minor place in the world's scheme.[1] Thought that does not lead to action is demoralizing, and one of the prime errors of the Victorian age was sentimentality: witness the beautiful thoughts and unpleasant characters of some great Victorian writers—though there are exceptions such as Swinburne in his prose, who bestowed all his unpleasantness upon the world. The curiosity that leads us to search out details of an admired author's life, and makes us regret that we know little of Shakespeare's life, is an unconscious wish to see thought come true in action. It is unsatisfactory to see a gulf fixed between life and thought—as in the well-known instance of Hume, who wrote sceptical treatises but admitted that his private religious views did not differ greatly from the orthodox; or Marx, who said that he was himself no Marxist; or John Bright, who made 'Angel of Death' speeches in Parliament and employed child labour in his mills. It is no unusual thing to see persons of great wealth and luxurious living calling themselves socialists. They have a host of ready arguments against selling all and giving to the poor, but the contrast is none the less unsatisfactory and savours of the King in *Hamlet*: 'May one be pardoned and retain the offence?' The great mystics—St. Francis of Assisi, St. Teresa, St. Catherine of Siena, and others—were not

[1] Bergson thinks that the natural enmity felt by the natives of one country for another would be purged by knowledge of its literature and consequent saturation with its spirit (*Les Deux Sources de la Morale et de la Rêligion*, 11th edn., p. 309).

solitary dwellers in desert or cloister but active in the busy world. Literature, like religion, is not an affair of the mind only but the whole personality. There is this in common between the upper and lower classes, between peasant and nobleman—and too often denied to the business and professional classes, outside writers, artists, and musicians—the power to convert thought into action, to live according to their philosophy.

The typical new-rich man gives his children an expensive education to advance them socially, but he looks on education as an external accomplishment or decoration—something that is put on and off like fine clothes, to impress the neighbours—not that which converts the will and effects a different manner of living. No doubt he would be proud to hear his son quote lines like Tennyson's

> 'Move upwards working out the beast,
> And let the ape and tiger die'.

To him that would be an instance of true culture, a return for the money which he had paid to the professors; yet he himself has reached his position by due enlargement of the internal ape and tiger, and if he thought that their suppression in his son would compromise the family business, he would immediately retract. The middle classes are called the backbone of a nation; only, be it remembered, this world is not a self-contained thing, its frontiers are open to eternity. The true quality of the mind appears as it travels further and further from the fact. Necessity compels the professional and business man to keep within the bounds of fact, to be governed by the standards of respectability and opinions of others. But it is only when the pull of fact relaxes its power and the mind takes off into space that we get originality. There are many intermediate stages in the ascent, beginning with the public-school man who dislikes conventionality and boredom but mistrusts what he calls eccentricity. Rome owed much of her early greatness to her senators whose genius was above all impersonal, and it has been recorded that not only did they act uniformly, whether individually or in a body, but that a hundred Roman senators once all dreamed the same dream.

We often hear people say with an air of superiority that they have learnt to look on things as they are. They merely admit themselves to be reverting to the beast and renouncing education and decency. The lower you descend in the moral, intellectual, and social scale, the more realistic do people become. This attitude of mind, during the first great European war, was said to be purely German,[1] though we are inclined to think that it has representatives in every country of the world. Education should teach us to see things through a veil of idealism and imagination.[2] Charlotte Brontë saw the Haworth curates as they were, and the result is Donne, Malone, and Sweeting of *Shirley*. She saw Heger as she wished him to be, and the result is Paul Emanuel of *Villette*. It is almost true to say that every profession or business deliberately destroys the work of education. Nowadays money is omnipotent, large fortunes are only made in business, and the ideal which everyone sets before himself and encourages his children to attain is success in business. Competition is more naked and unashamed in business than in the professions. Even in the past, education took longest to soften the hearts of the descendants of the successful business man. How much more so at present when there exists neither opportunity nor will to depart from jungle standards! The great ones of the earth are to be those for whom education has done and can do least. There will be no peace until Commercialism is exorcized with its fellow evil spirits—Nazism, Fascism, Communism. God-State, God-Proletariat, God-Mammon are the same. Their creed is that might is right, and material efficiency the aim of

[1] See a powerful article, *German Logic and its Results*, by Arthur E. P. Broome Weigall (*Fortnightly Review*, Oct. 1915).

[2] 'Society is a form of poetry' (Amiel).

education. One of Hitler's worst crimes was to close the universities and 'imprison the mind', but the business man who sneers at the university man for his 'useless' knowledge has the Nazi mentality. The pure money-maker is as far beyond education as he is beyond good and evil. Besides, the training for business, unlike the learned professions, is experience, not disinterested knowledge, and against this fundamental contradiction of self-annihilation in the cause of truth, which is the aim of all knowledge, as it is of all morality, and self-interest, self-assertion, and self-protection which are the aims of all business, there is no appeal. The successful business man who in outer things has become the equal of the great ones of the earth has nothing inner on which to base himself, and, being in a false position, never ceases to proclaim in self-defence the power of money. He is like Mammon, as depicted by Milton, who even before he fell with Satan's rout was blind to the beatific vision and walked in heaven with eyes bent downward upon the trodden gold of its pavement.

Flight from the fact has now to be reconciled with the statement that education is not fulfilled until it becomes action. Some persons maintain that quotation is bad taste—akin to ostentatious display of wealth. Landor remarked that a quoter is either ostentatious of his acquirements or doubtful of his cause. Here again is overstatement and shadow of truth. It means that education has not been entirely assimilated, has stayed in the conscious mind, not descended into the unconscious and gone forth in action. Plato prophesied the fairest destiny in the world hereafter for those who had practised in this world the virtues of moderation and justice by nature and habit, without philosophy or reason,[1] and this

[1] *Phaedo* 82, A-B. It must be admitted that in the *Republic* (X. 619, C) Plato seems to contradict this. He speaks of someone whose virtue was a matter of habit only, without philosophy. In Epistle VII he says that the doctrine of the Good cannot be written down and made a branch of study, but must be discovered by each one for himself (341, C–E).

accords with FitzGerald's praise of the English country gentleman who lived his education but did not talk about it. Some passages in the letters of Lord Chesterfield to his son are partially suited to the present discussion. He writes, 'Proverbial expressions and trite sayings are the flowers of the rhetoric of a vulgar man.' And again, 'A man of fashion never has recourse to proverbs and vulgar aphorisms, will use neither favourite words nor hard words.' Our ideals, we hope, are higher than to be men of fashion, yet it is true that most people, at least in their working philosophy, place good manners and good breeding at the head of mankind's achievement, above the conquests of brain and brawn, above politics and lost causes, above even the power of Mammon. 'Aristocrats corrupt our very messengers!' was the cry of indignation raised by a French revolutionary mob.[1] The most intellectual persons are not always the most untouched by spot of earth. They are self-taught and conscious of their knowledge and cleverness, as the new-rich are conscious of their possessions and the power of brain and character which has enabled them to overthrow their rivals.

The virtues of moderation and justice dear to Plato were practised by the country gentlemen whom FitzGerald extolled. The result of their lives of ease and leisure, removed from competition, was annihilation of self; they were conscious how insignificant a point in the infinite is the earthly ego: and here is the link between life and imagination. There are times when doing nothing is a form of action—to know, like Socrates, that we know nothing; like Shakespeare, that we are such stuff as dreams are made on; that this earth is a dissolving pageant wherein the part played by the greatest of us is not very great; that against the background of the universe our human peaks show but slightly.

[1] It is said that George Lansbury once warned his fellow Labour members of Parliament against friendship with Conservative members, lest their socialist principles should be weakened by contact with persons of charming manners.

Because the lives of the aristocracy and squirearchy of England were steeped in this semi-divine light, they were esteemed by the people as representatives of a higher order —midway between earth and heaven—and their manners and outlook on life were an ideal ever present as something that might be realized by the classes just below them. With their disappearance the world is thrown back into unlimited competition and the law of the strongest. The passing of an old order should make us search for an alternative, not try to stem the Atlantic. The virtues we regret were the result of leisure; and Talleyrand said that no one who had not lived before the Revolution could form an idea of the sweetness of life. Even if such leisure were now possible, it could not be enjoyed, for the world has become economically one, and no one cares to play, however gracefully, when he realizes that the majority of his fellow creatures are at work. Besides, the true background of aristocracy is the land, and now that the old country life, with its silence and seclusion and feudal tradition of service, has vanished, the possession of unearned money and absence of need to work would liker lead to decadence than spiritual growth. The problem is to use the imagination which once informed the lives of a privileged class and was part of their heritage, as a means of shortening the period of three generations which education requires to complete itself in the average family—to make a kind of Promethean theft of imaginative fire from the poets who live in the heaven of the sun and bestow it upon benighted mankind.

To distil this precious quality from literature into life, and so dematerialize the mind, is the practical office of reading. To attempt to define the inner spirit of a poet's work may seem like chasing the rainbow, yet imaginative, like mystical, experience is the same in all, and at least it will avoid that modern style which turns a critical essay into a scientific treatise with charts and diagrams. Saintsbury deprecated excessive method in literary criticism, and recalled that the greatest critical work of the ancient world, that of Longinus, had very little of it. Imaginative truth need not be moral truth, and it is lack of this perception that condemns to failure the whole vast body of modern German Shakespearian criticism, from Gervinus to Schücking. We hear German plaints that Bassanio was unworthy of Portia because he did not earn his own living, or objections that Antonio, with his friends and credit, could easily have raised money. In Rümelin's view Shylock would not have broken the law by taking *less* than his pound of flesh. Gervinus thinks that Shakespeare wrote the *Merchant of Venice* to show the true relation of man to property; in Ulrici's opinion his object was to show that the more you insist on the letter of the law the greater is the moral wrong. Schücking decides that the story of Lear is a breakdown rather than a development.[1] If we agree that imagination is the power to see a thing in its relation to the universe, the result is devaluation of the fact; but in removing the fact the fairies leave something very precious in its place—something that we would not exchange for Balak's house full of silver and gold.

Tennyson makes Tithonus say,

> 'A soft air fans the cloud apart; there comes
> A glimpse of that dark world where I was born.'

How far does the imaginative world exclude the real? How far, in frequenting the upper spaces of the imagination, can we forget the dark world of our birth? The German critics

[1] Here are two instances of German literalness from Carlyle's *Frederick* (Vol. III). The first is the death of the wife of George II of England: 'The dying Caroline recommended *him* to Walpole; advised his Majesty to marry again. "Non, j'aurai des maîtresses", sobbed his Majesty passionately' (p. 213). The second is at the last illness of King Frederick William of Prussia: 'In a certain German hymn . . . which they often sang to him, or along with him, as he much loved it, are these words, "Naked I came into the world, and naked shall I go." "No", said he, always with vivacity, at this passage; "not quite naked, I shall have my uniform on"' (p. 270).

of Shakespeare are stuck fast in the mud of earthly fact; a book like Rousseau's *Nouvelle Héloïse*, made up of airy nothings, has lost its appeal. What Jacob saw in Padan Aram was communication between earth and heaven. The problem is to recognize the earthly thing in its heavenly dress. We love the Falstaff of I *Henry IV*, but in life we would not love a person who told untruths and robbed travellers on the highway. The reason is that Falstaff by his intense enjoyment of life suggests to us a state of being where material possessions do not count and the true joy is the communion of minds. The core of Shakespeare's thought, I believe, is delight in human fellowship. It appears even through the passion of Romeo and Juliet, as when Juliet says,

> 'Or if thou think'st I am too quickly won,
> I'll frown and be perverse, and say thee nay,
> So thou wilt woo; but else, not for the world.
> In truth, fair Montague, I am too fond;
> And therefore thou may'st think my haviour light.
> But trust me, gentleman, I'll prove more true
> Than those that have more cunning to be strange.'

It makes Lear, who is fourscore and upward, anticipate with joy the companionship of Cordelia in prison. Even Macbeth regrets the 'troops of friends' from whom crime has severed him. Shakespeare omitted the unseen world, no doubt for dramatic reasons, but the human relations of men and women became mystic from the touch of his mind.

The lightened fact, not its annihilation, is the test of imaginative truth. The songs of Shakespeare, the music of Mozart, the pinnacles of a Gothic cathedral—all these have a lightness that makes them appear easy, as if any one of us could have done as well. I do not subscribe to the modern doctrine that the intellectual content of poetry is of no concern, though it has been vindicated in humorous fashion by Mr. T. S. Eliot. He says, 'The chief use of the "meaning" of a poem, in the ordinary sense, may be . . . to satisfy one habit of the reader, to keep his mind diverted and quiet, while the poem does its work upon him: much as the imaginary burglar is always provided with a bit of nice meat for the house dog'.[1] This world is only an illusion if judged as complete in itself, not as the stairway to heaven. It was no ill distinction that bad poetry means what it says, good poetry by its sound and movement suggests emotions that cannot be expressed by the meaning of words.[2] W. P. Ker said that you cannot compare Milton's *Paradise Lost* and Pepys's *Diary*, yet the very incongruity brings home to us the value of the *Diary*.[3] On such great authority I will venture to compare Virgil and Mrs. Hemans. If sincerity and deep feeling could make a poet, Mrs. Hemans would be supreme. She writes,

> 'Oh call my brother back to me,
> I cannot play alone,
> The summer comes with flower and bee,
> Where is my brother gone?'

And the poem concludes,

> 'Oh while my brother with me played,
> Would I had loved him more!'

We turn to the speech between Dido and her sister Anna in *Aeneid* IV, to the line,

> 'Anna refert, O luce magis dilecta sorori'.[4]

The sentiment is conventional, a formal compliment, but the sound and movement take us far beyond. All that we have ever heard or known of sisterly affection, the love of those who have grown up together from earliest years, the true meaning of home—all this is vaguely stirred up in our minds by the enchanting melody.

We will compare Virgil with a worthier rival, namely Milton, in this attempt to define experience of the universal

1 *The Use of Poetry and the Use of Criticism*, p. 151.

2 See Myers on Virgil. 3 *Collected Essays*, Vol. I, p. 109.

4 'Anna replies, O thou who art dearer to thy sister than the light.'

which is the goal of imagination. The despairing creed of certain Victorian agnostics that Nature was a machine controlled by iron laws, indifferent to the sufferings of living creatures, has been corrected by modern thinkers. The human mind, they argue, is the latest stage of evolution, and Nature protests against cruelty through ourselves. This cosmic emotion was long ago expressed by the poets, and by none more poignantly than Virgil. Milton writes in *Lycidas*,

> 'Ah me, whilst thee the shores and sounding seas
> Wash far away!'

The emotion here is academic—the melancholy of the scholar-poet twice removed from reality. Its original is the passage where the shade of the steersman Palinurus meets Aeneas in the lower world and tells him of his fate—how, having fallen from the ship at night, he succeeded in reaching Italy by swimming, but as he clung to the rock, the cruel inhabitants of the coast attacked and wounded and flung him back to drown. Then the agitation subsides, and there follows a line which for its majesty and its pathos is unrivalled throughout Virgil:

> 'Nunc me fluctus habet, versantque in litore venti.'[1]

This line comes to us charged with all the terror, the helplessness, and the resignation of man before the blind and awful forces of the universe.

If imagination is to see a thing in relation to the universal, and the result is devaluation of the fact, we ask what moral is to be drawn, how can we use it to reform our lives? We saw the late-born romantic betrayed by his memories of earth. He needs an effort to leave the busy world and dream his dream of beauty, and—to quote Montaigne—'nothing imprints anything so strongly on our memory as the desire to forget it'. For this reason the reputations of the Brontës

[1] 'Now my body is at the mercy of the waves, and the winds drive it from shore to shore.'

have been reversed, and Emily is preferred to Charlotte. Charlotte darkens the Yorkshire moors with the shadow of hope deferred and unrealized human longing; Emily exalts them into the playground of heaven. Many modern thinkers, and Dean Inge especially, tell us that mysticism is the core of religion; but for one person who attains the goal, a hundred can reach the halfway house of imagination. The first stage is learned ignorance, or negative action—to realize that we know nothing, to suppress the ego, to withhold opinion, to eschew argument; the second is the attempt to make every incident of our lives not self-centred but God-centred. The family of Jane Austen, one of the most refined in family history, followed the unwritten law never to argue. In the time of Dante and the Middle Ages courtesy was said to be an attribute of God. The faith of our new-rich friend in education would be shaken, as we hinted, were education to fulfil its ideal course and diminish the positive beliefs of his sons, and therefore their self-assertion and money-making capabilities. We will recall some of our instances to prove that things are not always what they seem, and that matter can be fined down in such a way as to make Falstaff's thefts seem a little thing compared with his joy. We remember Madame Grandet, preoccupied with the prices of things, defeated and disfigured by her struggle with earth, but safe at the last, made young again and beautiful, strangely altered and glorified in the presence of death.

The ideal of negative action may seem an impotent and lame conclusion, but passivity, which is not the same as inertia, is the beginning of knowledge; it was in such a condition that to St. Teresa came the beatific vision.[1] Nature works by rhythm, and wise passivity is the prelude to

[1] 'Genius is receptiveness' (A. E. Taylor, *Faith of a Moralist*, Vol. II, p. 91). See also A. C. Bradley's remarks on 'negation'. Man's spirit, he says, can only return to God 'through the deepest of all conflicts and negations . . . total denial of his finite being' (*A Miscellany*, pp. 136–7).

vigorous action. The greatest mystics have been the greatest doers, like Joan of Arc, or St. Bernard, reputed the busiest man of his day in Europe. The East still remains rapt in meditation, and it has been suggested that new faith to troubled Europe may come from India where live prophets and seers as great as any in the past. Man cannot exist without religion, and when he becomes dulled to the unseen world he worships things of sense. The modern idols of Nationalism, Communism, Nazism, Fascism witness to this, and in the absolute State, the absolute family, he is reverting to the practice of the ancient Romans. To fill the gap between true faith and present confusion, the society of the world's great writers is always open, and its entrance fee is the minimum of perseverance. A daily half-hour for a few years spent with some chosen books will change the moral centre of gravity. After one or two set-backs the student will be aware of a light that is not earthly moving upon the page. His progress will be like that of Dante, who felt no sensible motion as he rose through the spheres of heaven but knew that he was rising because the expression in the eyes of Beatrice had become more lovely. We conclude, therefore, that study of literature is not only for solitary musings, or to impress the world and promote feelings of superiority, but something to influence the whole of our reaction to life, to control our deeds and affect our behaviour to others in daily business, and, above all, something that has a definite part to play in the return to the Cross.

As the world is now ordered, with private profit-making as its leading motive, education cannot make those who conduct its business change their lives, though it may supply them with outer graces. Confucius taught that all reform begins with the individual, that he must first purify his heart, and to achieve this must think sincere thoughts, but sincere thinking is only attained through knowledge. Complete knowledge is impossible, because to know a thing we must know it in relation to everything else in the universe[1]; and therefore scientific knowledge, through its exclusions, is furthest from truth, and poetic knowledge is nearest, because by simile and metaphor it discovers unexpected relations between far-removed things, and suggests ultimate unification. It is usually said that the basis of poetry is emotion, that the poet differs from others by his greater sensitiveness, and is therefore not a trustworthy guide to life. The first part of this saying is true and the last untrue when it is understood that the emotion which inspires poetry must be intellectualized. The poet's duty is to make his finer sensitiveness the means to knowledge, and to subserve not overpower his intellect. The object of knowledge is best summed in the last line of the *Divine Comedy*: 'The love that moves the sun and all the stars'.[2] Poetry should be written on the principle of making clearer the working of this law in the present state of the world, and life should be lived so as to realize it on earth. Without knowledge, emotion, either in living or writing, may be merely personal, or wastefully outpoured on chance objects unrelated to the universal scheme. It is easy for a writer to show that he himself is moved, but hard to make his emotion the starting point of his thought, so that by discovering a likeness he may unite to the divine order something that hitherto had seemed to lie outside it. In life the true philanthropist has often to resist appeals to his mercy and appear hard, because he knows that indiscriminate giving does not forward the great event. Emotion counts not in its disturbance of the individual but in its justification of a place in God's universe by revealing a new-found land of interconnections. The light of the furthest star that adds to the radiance of the heavens is more impressive than the glare of a burning house. It is here that imagination becomes the teacher of reality, and that art serves religion.

[1] See above, p. 16 note.

[2] Dante derived this and many other thoughts from Boethius.

THE APPROACH TO FAITH

THE APPROACH TO FAITH

There are certain passages in Shakespeare that make us worship him, as Bradley said, and surely this is one of them:

> 'Heaven doth with us as we with torches do,
> Not light them for themselves; for if our virtues
> Did not go forth of us, 'twere all alike
> As if we had them not. Spirits are not finely touched
> But to fine issues. . . .[1]

If we wish to be convinced of the existence of a world hereafter, we must play our part in this world, and our first duty is to work, to develop to the full such faculties as we have. Great men of action are not sceptics, because they have mastered their environment, and man is not complete apart from his environment; but poets and philosophers frequently are sceptics—including the greatest speculative genius of all time, Leonardo da Vinci—because thoughts have a way of multiplying themselves till they exceed their corresponding objects in the outer world. Marlborough, Wellington, Chatham, Pitt, Napoleon, Foch—these men were no sceptics. Carlyle tells how Napoleon, on board ship, silenced the *philosophes* who had satisfactorily proved among themselves there was no God. 'Who made all that?' he said, pointing to the sea and sky. Frederick the Great was inclined to scepticism, but of all leaders of men he was the most interested in speculative thought, and a producer of quantities of inferior verse; yet it is on record that 'he could not abide atheism'.

[1] *Measure for Measure*, I. 1.

Pater once remarked on the sadness which fills the human mind when its thoughts wander far from what is here and now; and of the rush of homesickness with which the thought of death presents itself.[1] He was writing of the pagan world, but his words would apply to many an artist or poet or thinker in post-medieval times. This was not so in the past when the totalitarian Catholic Church organized the world in its relationships like one large family, but since the Reformation the framework of institutional religion has grown less and less substantial, till in these modern times it has been nearly battered out of recognition by wars and revolutions and industrial upheavals and materialistic ideologies. Some of the Renaissance artists (once more on the authority of Pater) were content to live uneventful, secluded lives, because their minds were filled with heavenly visions; but even Dante, at a time when the Church predominated, would have preferred the life of action. One cannot imagine Chaucer or Spenser dissatisfied with their whole-time art, yet they were by no means separated from the world of affairs and political missions. Shakespeare, always the ideal, combined the two, and amply vindicated Dr. Johnson's saying that no one but a fool ever wrote except for money. Milton's conscience first troubled him when he was travelling in Italy at the time of the outbreak of the Civil War. He postponed *Paradise Lost*, and engaged in politics and violent controversies that left permanent scars in his moral nature.

As time passed on, and the spread of knowledge levelled up individuals and reduced the height of the peaks and made overwhelming poetic genius more rare, the cry of the spirit grew louder. The sceptical philosophy of the eighteenth century is reflected in the sufferings of the poets. Gray wrote of the approach of the inevitable hour, and how the paths of glory lead but to the grave; and all his life he endured low spirits and melancholy. Arnold explained Gray's scanty

[1] *Renaissance*, pp. 200–1.

production by the fact that he was a genuine poet born in an age of prose; but it is even more significant that in the eighteenth century men of letters began to lose touch with active life. Dryden and Pope flourished on patronage and attained a somewhat artificial prosperity; Gray lived a life of ease secure in his Cambridge fellowship, and though he produced little original work he became immensely learned, but the exertions of his mind found no sufficient counterpart in the world without. Dr. Johnson's sufferings from hypochondria are notorious, and they were intensified in later years when he had surmounted his early difficulties and obtained a pension. He himself sorrowfully tells us that he was indolent, and had to make painful efforts to work at his edition of Shakespeare and biographies of the poets. Among Boswell's many amusing sketches is one of Johnson acting as executor and giving himself airs of importance at this contact with practical life. If anyone lived blamelessly it was Cowper, but he made the great refusal, and obtained the comforts of family life without its responsibilities. Positive, not negative, qualities count in the world, and therefore Napoleon with all his faults and crimes has never lacked admirers and apologists, because he was a great actor in the affairs of the world. There are few records of spiritual torture equal to what Cowper endured, and his last letters are almost too painful to read. Sheridan supplies a good instance of the gap between thought and action in the artist. His speech against Warren Hastings was the beginning of his Parliamentary reputation. In later years he met Hastings and informed him that he had always respected him, and only political necessity inspired the speech. 'Will you make that public?' replied the man of affairs, and Sheridan was put to confusion.

Of the poets of the nineteenth century, though it would be possible to draw up a list of evenly matched sceptics and believers, it would be hard to point to one who attained true peace. Coleridge had to use so many subtle arguments to justify his belief that Carlyle dismissed his theology as 'Coleridgean moonshine'. Wordsworth is often quoted as a type of orthodoxy, but he too suffered from hypochondria, was fearful in old age, anxious about the condition of the country, and obsessed by the thought of a coming catastrophe. Keats was a sceptic, and no ray of hope visited him in his last tragic illness. Carlyle affirms in *Sartor* that he experienced what is called 'conversion', but the effect does not seem to have been lasting, and the letters and journals of his whole life bear witness to an uneasy mind. It is hard to think of Edward FitzGerald apart from the *Omar*, and his last words to the well-meaning clergyman who discoursed to him on religion were, 'You need not repeat this visit'. The lives of Shelley and Byron were disastrous, and each in his fashion scandalized the orthodox by the expression of his religious views. It is possible to cite Tennyson, Browning, and Meredith as instances of believers, but it is characteristic of the later nineteenth century that they should be always on the defensive. Tennyson said that after his marriage the peace of God entered into his soul, but he was eternally preoccupied by the cosmic problem. William Morris was haunted throughout life by the thought of death; over and over again he puts into the minds of his lovers, who have at last attained each other, the thought that only the knowledge of death interrupts their perfect bliss. Swinburne professed that he had found happiness in the prospect of annihilation; and hope was not conspicuous in Arnold's theology. Nearer our own time, Bridges alone stands out as a believer among a host of sceptics headed by Thomas Hardy and A. E. Housman. Their mood is crystallized for ever in William Watson's poem *The Great Misgiving*.

It is impossible to resist the conclusion that the poet, ever something of an exile on earth, in modern times must pay a double penalty for devotion to his art—exile from God as well as man. The Reformation, the French Revolution, the break-up of feudalism, the beginning of industrialism, the decline of country life and concentration of men in large towns, the invention of the railway and the internal-combustion engine: all these things are milestones on the road that leads away from poetry, and force it to occupy a more and more narrow corner of the world, despite Romantic and other revivals. 'Anxiety is the enemy of poetry', as Newman said; and how shall the modern poet sing the Lord's song in a strange land? When the world was a family, and looked upon God as the Father of all, property was like His patrimony, and class distinctions were what He willed. It sufficed a man to do his duty in the state into which he was born. Earth's inhabitants now are like castaways on a desert island; each is valued according to his power to serve his fellows in the struggle with nature, not according to the virtues of his ancestors. Tradition dies hard, but the man who does no work is not now taken seriously by others. Bernard Shaw says that 'all men are in a false position in society until they have realized their possibilities, and imposed them on their neighbours'.[1] Cecil Rhodes, when willing large sums to Oxford, alluded to the dons as 'children', who live apart from the world and know nothing of business. It is no disparagement to the immense learning and industrious lives of most university dons to say that a position like theirs is a kind of compromise with life. Their living once assured, the balance inclines from action to speculation.[2] Dr. Johnson's remark about the material rewards of literature has been already cited, and all this sounds like judgment by results and worship of success; but there is something in men's

[1] Preface to *Immaturity* (1921).

[2] Sir Charles Oman's description of Prof. York Powell is typical. York Powell, he says, was 'an untiring browser in every field of knowledge, but a very scanty producer of any finished work'. He 'neglected all appointments and broke many engagements'. It is to the point that by his own wish he was buried without religious ceremony. Oman concludes: 'We defiled past the deep pit in Summertown Cemetery in blank silence—and that was all: it was very depressing' (*Memories of Victorian Oxford* (1941), pp. 204–6).

inarticulate wisdom, and Plato did say that to be thought well of or not by the world is no small thing, and the many are not so wrong in judging who are bad and who are good as they are removed from the nature of virtue in themselves, and even bad men have a divine instinct that guesses well.[1]

Wordsworth conceived loftily of the poet's vocation, and fulfilled it, yet did not find peace. Cowper was almost a saint, yet few men have suffered as he did. Tolstoy, well served by two of the world's greatest gifts—genius and high birth—quarrelled with the world. Tolstoy was more poet than novelist—like Charlotte Brontë, another victim of hypochondria—for the novelist is usually of a more robust mental and nervous constitution than the pure poet or artist. The novelist has vested interests in the world, and he may be called a link between the artist and the people. Scott was untroubled by religious doubt, and not only was his power of work prodigious but also his capacity for social and other pleasures, so that there were no desert spaces in his inner life. The outer world played a good part with Dickens and Thackeray—the life of the streets with Dickens, and clubs and drawing-rooms with Thackeray. Of Balzac, thanks to the enormous power of his imagination, the outer and inner world were one, and the characters of his books more real to him, during their execution, than the persons about him.

It is when we turn to the lesser artist that the tragedy deepens, for of all persons born under the sun he is the most disabled. We are told that asylums and mental homes are largely filled with persons who have the artistic temperament without the power. Life should be creative, and the lesser artist can only create fitfully or at long intervals, and is therefore outside life, and when he carries his wares to market no buyers frequent his stall. Charles Lamb visited Oxford in the Long Vacation, and, strolling about the streets, pleased himself with the fancy that he was Master of

[1] *Laws*, XII. 950, B.

Arts or Seraphic Doctor; or rose with the chapel bell and dreamt that it rang for him. FitzGerald lamented that he spent his mature years reading books which everyone else had read at school. Such is the lot of the lesser artist, not living but playing at life—and so the comfort of faith is denied him. To be among men but not of them is a solitude more deathlike than the Arctic spaces.[1] If Coleridge, whose first-rate powers were destroyed by opium, could write, 'All Nature seems at work. . . . And I the while, the sole unbusy thing',[2] how much more does the lesser artist feel his position in a creative world where even the greatest writers are ill at ease. Perhaps it is not fair to speak of Lamb and FitzGerald as lesser artists, considering the quality of their best work, but the letters of FitzGerald in his unproductive years tell us much of the species. It is true that such a man does not grow old, and remains childlike to the end, because the world will not trust him with material responsibilities, but the gain is far outweighed by the loss, and in the climacteric years of life he has no respite from the saddest thoughts.

We learn most from poets and artists because their self-expression is fuller, and the spirit of an age shows clearest in its highest evolved persons, but the same mental life is shared in by the many. The soul-sickness of the last centuries is not the privilege of a few chosen spirits, nor is it a mark of high culture, as some have naïvely considered. The punctual office-worker is less unspiritual than some superior persons think; he has at least stilled his doubts, though his work may be only preparatory. He will tell you that he has no time to think about religion: in which he shows self-deception and

[1] Professor John Baillie quotes the saying of St. Thomas Aquinas that knowledge of God comes only through 'the humiliations of the material order'. He continues, 'This means, first, that the knowledge of God is withholden from those who keep themselves aloof from the *service* of their fellows. . . . And this is indeed a blessed provision by which God makes my knowledge of Himself pass through my brother's need' (*Our Knowledge of God*, p. 179).

[2] *Work without Hope.*

confusion of thought. 'Work is worship' is an old saying, and *acedia*, or weariness of life, was a sin in the Middle Ages, and most prevailed in monasteries where life was purely contemplative. The answer to those who deride men's activities and their absorption in apparently small things, and who profess to take long views and point out that these things which interest now will be of little value in a few years when we shall all be dead, is that the busy man is engaged in the important task of making his own soul.[1] To cultivate one's garden has become a proverb, and Charlotte Brontë, at the climax of her inspiration, the visit to the confessional in *Villette*, makes the priest tell Lucy Snowe (her thinly disguised self) that a mind so tossed can only find refuge in the regular discharge of pious actions.

The shock given by Darwin to man's self-estimation was the greatest since Copernicus decentralized the Earth, but it merely accelerated what the French Revolution had begun. The tactics of the Victorians, who had inherited a religious tradition, were ostrich-like. Feeling ill at ease without religion, they concentrated upon their work which brought them temporary relief, and when work is pursued for its own sake it leads to the pursuit of money for its own sake, with inevitable deterioration of character. The heavenly lights had not quite gone out in Victorian days, and the business man justified himself by the teaching of Calvin. Sloth was a greater sin than covetousness, poverty was a disgrace, pleasure and luxury were to be shunned. The Old Testa-

[1] 'Scientific research is the modern form of the religious life. It gives courage and fundamental serenity. It is the securest refuge from the distresses of the human soul' (H. G. Wells, *The Work, Wealth, and Happiness of Mankind*, p. 84). Bergson writes: '. . . l'homme strictement inséré dans le cadre de son métier ou de sa profession, qui serait tout entier à son labeur quotidien, qui organiserait sa vie de manière à fournir la plus grande quantité et la meilleure qualité possible de travail, s'acquitterait généralement *ipso facto* de beaucoup d'autres obligations. La discipline aurait fait de lui un honnête homme' (*op. cit.*, p. 99).

ment taught that virtue brought reward in this world, and wealth was a sign of God's favour. The typical Victorian business man has been immortally distinguished by Thackeray in old Osborne of *Vanity Fair*; and the characters of misers drawn by Balzac were prophetic of the great part money was to play in the nineteenth century.

No one can have worshipped money less than Carlyle, and yet his Gospel of Work was not truly based. He also was ostrich-like, and worked to forget himself and escape the hounds that were upon his track. He admitted that he only felt truly alive when he was at work, though he condemned literature as a profession, calling it the 'despicable Author Trade', or the 'haven of windy aspirations', and did not resign himself until his several attempts to enter active life had failed. The most memorable of his historical portraits is Louis XV, 'whose life only became a reality in the moment of death'.[1] Ennui, he said, was the most hopeful sign in the lives of those who were surfeited with money; and he warned them it would pursue them 'if they mounted to the stars and made yacht voyages under the belts of Jupiter, or stalked deer on the ring of Saturn'.[2] Burke likewise commiserated the 'palled satiety of those whose desires even are anticipated, and no obstacle interposed between wish and accomplishment'.[3] Carlyle's father said that 'man was created to work, not to speculate or feel or dream'; and he was a greater man than Carlyle himself, in that he was never visited by doubt and put his theories into practice.[4]

The Medievalists were nearer the truth than the Victorians when they insisted that it was not the work that counted but the spirit in which it was done. The best among the Victorians applied themselves to work because it was the halfway house toward the relief of doubt; with the worst, the

[1] *French Revolution.* [2] *Pamphlets: Jesuitism.*

[3] *Reflections on the French Revolution.*

[4] 'Work is my sore burden, but it is also my great resource. I eat my heart out when I am not up to the neck in work' (Sainte-Beuve).

spirit was forgotten and a man's work was judged by its money-producing result. Riches, said Bacon, are only despised by those who despair of them; and in the opinion of Mr. Aldous Huxley, 'extreme poverty can also be a needle's eye'.[1] Now that the human race has been temporarily dismissed from God's presence, and men face each other in the world's arena, the possession of earned money is a symbol that a man has proved himself. That one who does not earn his living, who, in Tolstoy's phrase, 'is born to be comforted by the labour of others', is looked askance at by his fellows, and he doubts his own right to exist. It was not so in the past, and it may not be so in the future; and Marx was at least right in contending that man is alienated from himself and his work by private property, as we see from the dehumanizing effect on the Victorians. According to Mr. Huxley, 'the ideal of the scholar and the gentleman originated among the slave-owning philosophers of Athens and Ionia',[2] and this suggests a reproach; but it must be admitted that the hereditary aristocracies of all races and ages have produced some of humanity's finest specimens, and this is specially true of the English aristocracy in later times, which reconquered its position by means of war and statesmanship, when the Reform Bill of 1832 had abolished privilege. Now, however, the tide in the affairs of men has turned, and it looks as if the issue from the Slough of Despond depends on work.

Carlyle likewise corrected our estimate of the ambition of great men. The last thing a great man wishes, he contended, is to outshine others and get the world to acknowledge his gifts and claims; but what he does rightly wish is to develop the powers which nature has implanted in him.[3] Ambition is so far good as it leads to self-development, but it must not be endless, or it will find no counterpart in the external world. The spirit of Piccarda was content to remain in the

[1] *Ends and Means*, p. 162. [2] *Op. cit.*, p. 203.
[3] *Heroes: Cromwell.*

Heaven of the Moon, and desired no further advancement lest such desire should conflict with the will of God.[1] Burke, in the passage already cited, remarks how the thoughts of those whose material wants are already supplied 'range without limit, and are diversified by infinite combinations in the wild and unbounded regions of imagination'. It is an old story that the gardener who has created a garden looks upon it as his own property far more than that of his employer who merely pays the bills. George III, when his head gardener died, said to his second man, 'Now you and I can do as we like!' From all this we gather that if we wish to attain faith and be re-admitted to God's presence, we must first conquer our material environment; but we must not work only to gain temporary relief from doubt, still less to make more and more money, but with the object of developing our powers and so placing ourselves in right relation to the universe.[2] In the words of Dr. Arnold (following St. Paul) when praying for a blessing upon daily work, we must do it 'in faith and heartily, as to the Lord and not unto men'.

The millions who flock to their daily toil and tell you they have no time to think about religion do not suffer consciously from doubt, though the struggle is postponed more than concluded. As Professor John Baillie says, 'God may be dwelling in their hearts incognito'; and with great impressiveness he proceeds to show that such faith is not complete.[3] Nor is it true that every kind of work brings peace; but rather was it a Victorian belief that any work which produced money was better than no work. Unbelief spreads fastest in the great cities where civilization exacts from man purely mechanical work: the tending of machines, the

[1] Dante: *Paradiso*, III. 64–87. Dante also says that 'nobleness' is the perfection in each thing of its proper nature (*Convivio*, IV. 16).

[2] 'The seer does not abstain from the work of the world but does it with his eyes fixed on the eternal'; 'The way to a higher life is normally through the world' (S. Radhakrishnan, *Eastern Religions and Western Thought*, pp. 97, 380).

[3] *Op. cit.*, p. 62.

repetition of the same action hour after hour, the making of parts with no reference to the completed whole. Such work is uncreative and leaves the mind unoccupied, and boredom is a foretaste of annihilation.[1] It is in creative work, in discovering in the outer world something that answers to the movements of his mind, that man is aware of the rhythm of the universe, and begins to make his soul and conquer boredom and annihilation. The soul is of God, and mystics tell us that in that world beyond, of which they have first-hand knowledge, there is no such thing as time but all is eternal Now.[2] We are happiest when we are most unconscious of time, and careworn in proportion as we feel time strictly as succession. Partings are the most painful things on earth, when everything is done, and there remains but to watch the clock. Louis XVI endured a parting scene of two hours with his family on the eve of his execution, and promised to revisit them next morning before he went forth to the guillotine, but he did not keep his promise. The soul of him who is conscious of time only as succession is dead. So was it with Macbeth, who killed his own soul when he killed Duncan. He reflects,

> 'For Banquo's issue have I filed my mind;
> For them the gracious Duncan have I murdered;
> Put rancours in the vessel of my peace
> Only for them. . . .'

[1] Mr. F. L. Lucas writes, 'Creation—be it only of a hencoop—seems to me half the secret of the good life. It is the sterile, uncreative, critical, or merely absorbent mind that is cursed like the barren fig-tree of Israel. The mentally passive are on their way to become mental patients' (*The Decline and Fall of the Romantic Ideal*, p. 152). Cf. B. H. Streeter: 'Whoever elects to live a constructive and creative life is living in harmony with the Power behind the Universe' (*The Buddha and the Christ*, pp. 254–5).

[2] 'Eternity is not time prolonged to infinity: it is the negation of time, something without duration, without successiveness; a Now that remains unchanging, with no past and with no future' (Edwyn Bevan, *Symbolism and Belief*, p. 83).

He cannot enjoy the present, but thinks only of the future; and thoughts which deal exclusively with the future are inevitably stayed by the blind alley of death. When he hears that Lady Macbeth is dead, he exclaims,

> 'She should have died hereafter;
> There would have been a time for such a word.'

The sadness that Pater attributed to the pagan mind when its thoughts wander far from what is here and now is universally true. Bertrand Russell says somewhere that the apprehension of death and probable annihilation need not detract from our enjoyment of life; but Professor Macneile Dixon is nearer the truth, that 'to foresee the end of happiness poisons the springs of happiness'.[1] FitzGerald was always prevented from wholeheartedly enjoying a friend's visit by anticipations of the friend's departure. To be conscious of the passage of time, that every minute, hour, day, week, month, season, year is bringing us nearer to death, that our years are steadily diminishing, that time passes faster and faster as we grow older, that the one thing we know for certain is that we shall die, as so many of our friends have died, and that death is a sleep from which there is no waking, a night which has no morrow, and to realize the meaning of the word 'never': the onset of thoughts like these does indeed make the hair of our flesh stand up, as did the spirit that passed before the face of Eliphaz the Temanite. Nothing in *Ecclesiastes* strikes such a chill as the saying how man goeth to his *long* home, and the days of darkness shall be many.[2]

Fortunately for the human race there is escape from this hell; it is only the few, without work or human ties, who encounter its full blast; though there have been periods, such

[1] *The Human Situation*, p. 86.

[2] Sir John Squire writes: 'Reconciled Bertram might be to Helena—but which of them would die first, and how would the other die? Married Portia might be to Bassanio, yet death has no truck with ducats' (*Shakespeare as a Dramatist*, p. 127).

as the later centuries of the western Roman Empire, or the court of Louis XV, when men's hearts have failed them. Louis, as Carlyle tells us, had the kingliest abhorrence of death, and never let it be mentioned in his presence, yet sometimes he perversely stopped his carriage at a cemetery and asked how many graves had been made lately. The majority of men are absorbed in earning their living, and of women in organizing their households, and when these primal duties are done, come other duties—to country, friends, society, the poor—in varying degrees of compulsion. From the energy put forth in these activities souls, or at least half-souls, are made and doubt is stilled; and the reason why the possessors of these souls or half-souls take seriously apparently small things is because the prize they contend for is immortality. As Homer said, when Achilles was pursuing Hector round the walls of Troy, they were not striving for beast of sacrifice or oxhide, the usual prize of a race, but for the life of Hector. The mistake is not to recognize that our duties, our activities, our pleasures even, have a sacred meaning: for there is something divine in the outer world which corresponds with the movements of our own minds.[1] An intellectual interest between persons is a bond that unites, but if these persons have suffered together the shocks of life, the bond is stronger. This explains why it is possible only to understand fully those of the same generation. The American A. J. Mahan wrote of 'the searching tests of common life'—alluding to the difficulty people find

[1] 'The mind of man has found in the very structure of the universe something deeply akin to itself' (D. S. Cairns, *The Riddle of the World*, p. 145). 'Can a universe which thought can so handle be mindless, without any affinity to the mind of man?'; 'Science does show us a correspondence, ever closer and wider, between the object known and the subject knowing' (Alfred E. Garvie, *The Christian Belief in God*, pp. 283–4, 287). 'Intellectual growth is a perpetually fuller responsiveness to the truth of the environment'; '. . . the recognition by mind of itself or of what is akin to it in its object' (William Temple, *Nature, Man and God*, pp. 128–9, 385).

in living together. It is because in daily happenings outer predominates over inner, and the mortified spirit cries out.

It is by the interaction of the inner self with the outer fact that we attain reality. Knowledge by itself leads nowhere; it is with applied knowledge that we approach the mystery, that we create; and the greater our difficulties the better for ourselves.[1] If this world is the vale of soul-making, we must plumb its depths, not glide over its surface, as do those to whom life offers no resistance, whose wants are automatically satisfied, who can indulge every whim without counting the cost, and who therefore feel the successive nature of time, as the empty years shrink before them, and are haunted by the fear of death.[2] A fact is sacred, and fiction has cousinship to lying, said Carlyle; and he regretted that neither Shakespeare nor Goethe wrote history, because Shakespeare's fact is more admirable than his fiction. We need but examine our own past to realize the sacredness of fact, especially in our dealings with those friends who are now beyond recall. There are certain memories which we account gains and possessions for ever because there were facts to correspond; certain others that haunt us like insubstantial ghosts—sins of omission, good intentions, might-have-beens which were never embodied in fact. Persons who boast that they do not take life seriously because it is short are merely confessing that they themselves are outside life. Man is not complete in himself but in interaction with his environment; he is placed in this world, and until he find something in its outer reality to correspond with his own soul, he is but half alive. To

[1] 'The law of polarity was for Heraclitus the supreme principle of the Cosmos. All energies had their contraries, and from the strain their opposition engendered the world had arisen. In a word, no oppositions, no world'; 'To our preposterous race obstacles are the breath of life' (Macneile Dixon, *op. cit.*, pp. 199, 232).

[2] 'Your easy chair is your great breeder of melancholia' (Macneile Dixon, *op. cit.*, p. 223). 'To live is to conquer incessantly; one must have the courage to be happy. I turn in a vicious circle; I have never had clear sight of my true vocation' (Amiel).

master the contents of a book is to add to and receive something from our environment, like systole and diastole, so that thereafter a part of ourselves persists in that book. We think of Chatham wearing the conquests of India and Canada like a mighty cuirass round his personality; of Wellington similarly fortified with Peninsula and Waterloo victories. Surely these men have a share in reality denied to the poet whose works remain in manuscript.

The task of the educationist should be to teach the young to search their hearts and find out that type of garden which they can best cultivate: and 'cultivation' need not be taken in a metaphorical sense, for there is no life more creative than that which contacts with earth. We can learn much from the peasant who ploughs the earth and sows, and gathers in the harvest, who sees his children grow up upon the land, who reads the Bible and attends the village church. If any such remain, untouched by the vices of the town, surely the civilizations of the world can show no better life. To know nature you must work with her, and so be drawn into her rhythm, not only contemplate her beauty.[1] The word 'tourist' has a sound of scorn, for the tourist looks and passes on and neither gives to nor receives from earth; he is unlike the ploughman or shepherd, and therefore outside the mystery of earth.

When hero-worship yielded to snobbishness, the world moved one step lower, for the hero is like the representative of God on earth. Not that snobbishness is entirely evil, for there is something mystical in ancient lineage and perfect manners, and lives which, having escaped competition for centuries, are raised above sordid cares. Even the airs of heaven could not winnow from Dante his pride of race.[2]

[1] Jaques Maritain quotes the peasant's saying reported by Proudhon, 'When I turn my furrows I feel like a king' (*True Humanism*, p. 159). Cf. Radhakrishnan: 'They (the peasants) had a hope in their hearts, a spark of poetry in their lives, an element of mystery in their make-up' (*op. cit.*, p. 38).

[2] *Paradiso*, XVI. 1–6.

It is by Mammon-worship that we revert to the beast, and develop realism and power-politics. Man cannot settle his affairs without God, and when he loses God, the stages of descent to worship of power and Mammon are inevitable. This world becomes for him a totalitarian place, and he values his work, his family, his home, his friends, his country, for their own sake, instead of as lamps to lighten his path into the presence of God.[1] If the world is ever to be raised out of its present trough of depression, there must be a fore-gleam of this spiritual truth. There is much latent faith in man, and it proves itself, with or against his will, through action which is forced upon him. The world could not exist if it were largely composed of individuals who were conscious that every day brought them nearer to the grave, as at the court of Louis XV.

Nor was Pascal right in commiserating mankind for finding no better solution of the problem of eternity than deliberately dismissing it from thought. Man, at least unconsciously, struggles to secure his half-immortality on earth not only by work but in his social relations with his fellow men. All those things which seem small and worthless in themselves, when we look back on a life that is over, were not so once. The last impression of Boswell's *Life of Johnson* on Edward FitzGerald was that all those people who spoke and acted so busily had passed away. But their wishes and strivings and interests and attempts to please were so much material out of which they made their souls. The line of Chaucer,

'Allas, departynge of our compaignye!'[2]

[1] 'We have tried to humanize our experience, to take man as the measure of all things, and now we are fast losing faith in man' (F. R. Barry, *The Relevance of Christianity*, p. 112). Dr. W. R. Matthews traces the decay of the desire for immortality to 'man's longing for the secure and settled, and utter dependence on the social environment'; 'The collectivized individual finds it intolerable to think of himself as reft from his social group' (*Essays in Construction*, pp. 208–9).

[2] *Knight's Tale*, 2774.

was spoken by the dying knight, but it is not only death that dissolves social groups, though the effect is like death, and the truth that emerges is the reality of man's social environment and its necessity for his soul. We know how vain is often the attempt to retain old friends when the complex social organization in which each one had a place has shifted, and mind is left alone with mind.

Charlotte Brontë wrote that 'people who are only in each other's company for amusement, never really like each other so well, or esteem each other so highly, as those who work together, and perhaps suffer together'.[1] Most of the love scenes in her books take place in the schoolroom; and it is a timely reminder that even enjoyment must be striven for, that to be passive is to be but half-fulfilled. Man must work to secure the enjoyment which is part of that environment which he must conquer, and which the Victorians curtailed lest it should impede money-making. The prayer has survived of Earl Brihtnoth (A.D. 991), 'O God, I thank Thee for all the joy I have had in life'. 'Asceticism extinguishes man's creative nature', writes Nicolas Berdyaev[2]; and Stopford Brooke noted that not a single original thought was expressed by F. W. Robertson in the years when, in order to spare more money for charity, he denied himself all but the barest necessities of life. It is the man with positive, not negative, virtues who now plucks immortality from the ruins of the time. Unselfishness, self-sacrifice, however beautiful, are looked upon as womanly rather than manly virtues; and thrift is the lowest of the virtues because it is negative. The world, on the whole, has forgiven Napoleon because he was a consummate doer, though he might indeed say with Dante's Manfred, 'My sins were horrible'.[3]

Belief apart from action, if not impossible, is at least valueless, for mere intellectual assent means nothing. Several modern thinkers use almost identical language in describing

[1] *Professor*, Ch. XXIII. [2] *Spirit and Reality*, p. 94.
[3] *Purgatorio*, III. 121.

the limitations of reason.[1] Now that the world is plunged in chaos, and all links with the past and traditions are broken, the immediate task is to develop our week-day soul, and become so far immortal as not to be painfully conscious of time as succession. Religious mania, or exotic beliefs, or over-anxious attention to forms and ceremonies are the resource of those who wish to believe but are without work and therefore without a centre of experience in this world. This lack is frequently the cause why persons become converts to other religions, or of the adoption by western Europeans of Mohammedanism or Hinduism or Buddhism, or of belief in fantastic superstitions: in other words, by forcing the mind to undertake violent exertions and gymnastics before it can approach the unseen. It was because Saul's prayers to God were unanswered that he sought the Witch of Endor. If the present world-fever does burn itself out, if the nations settle down in peace, and the worst contrasts of wealth and poverty are removed, a new social hierarchy may emerge when leisure may be neither a reproach among men nor a cause of spiritual distress to its possessor, because the place which a man fills in the thoughts of others is part of his environment. There are certain virtues which can only be acquired by leisure and adequately

[1] 'Proof rests upon nothing else than experiences which speak for themselves' (Macneile Dixon, *op. cit.*, p. 275). 'The reason is a secondary process . . . because it must have material to work upon. . . . It cannot go out into the invisible to discover new material for itself to work upon' (J. D. Beresford, *What I Believe*, p. 68). 'Reason is not so much the instrument for the discovery of truth as the faculty by which we test alleged truth. . . . All our most fundamental beliefs come from experience' (W. R. Matthews, *The Christian Belief in God*, p. 75). Prof. de Burgh warns us against confining reason to logic. He writes, 'Is it reasonable to charge a faith that thus succeeds in harmonizing experience, with illusion? When taken, as it needs must be, not as a momentary act but as the ruling principle of a life, faith is found to satisfy, by its issue in consistent behaviour, the very test by which the psychologist discriminates authentic from illusory apprehensions' (*op. cit.*, p. 19).

developed by inheritance—such as moderation in the use of power and money. The suffering brought on Europe by gangster politicians makes us recall Curzon's saying, that aristocracy may yet have useful work to do in the world: although the aristocrat is being parted from the land, which was his means of interacting with his environment. The success of the visit of the King and Queen to Canada and the United States in the summer of 1939 proves that the idea of the divine nature of kingship persists even in the New World. The Commune of 1871 made Flaubert revise his opinions—as it did many other French intellectuals—and elevate 'race' to the same height as 'intelligence' and education. Hope is eternal, and it is tempting to think that the downward course of the centuries can go no further, that mankind's darkest hour struck in September 1939, that such things may come to pass as closer union of the English-speaking races, a federalized Europe, freer trade, State control of prices, and international agreement that the working week of all hired workers, whether with hand or brain, shall not exceed forty-four hours—and then there will be an end of totalitarianism, unemployment, Mammon-worship, unrestricted competition, and all the harpies that have lately preyed on the human soul. For the present let us recognize that man is wrongly related to his environment, and in this world, the vale of soul-making, the wrong must be righted, for knowledge of the unseen world comes only through mastery of the seen.[1]

If stable governments and institutions return, and new traditions are founded, the artist also may find a place in the social organization. For centuries his position in the world has been growing precarious, and he has tended more and more to make the great refusal and decline material responsibilities. Even Wordsworth ended his days as an alarmed conservative, well knowing that if ruin threatened he could

[1] Cf. Granville-Barker on Hamlet: 'If man's mind cannot master the mortal world, what chance has it of mysteries beyond?'

stir no finger to avert it and must play the part of passive onlooker. The respect shown even by the great artist for the average man of action is a frequent phenomenon. 'Your pure man of letters often has a morbid love of mere *force*', wrote Saintsbury.[1] Newman was surrounded by intellectual inferiors whom he loved and respected. Samuel Butler, who was betrayed by the friend whom he had trusted and benefited, illustrates a remark of Coleridge's on the indiscreet friendships sometimes formed by men of genius, who are conscious of their own weakness and ready to believe others stronger than themselves.

Where the artist is on equal terms is in his personal relations, and he is apt to be longingly retrospective, to dwell much upon the incidents of his childhood or schooldays, when the emotional environment was supreme, when he had a definite place in the world, before he became a wanderer on its surface, even to be consumed with a passion for the past, like Rousseau. Love may be his supreme experience, as with Browning; or the loss of a loved one may shatter his whole existence, as with Dr. Johnson's incurable sorrow for his wife, or Carlyle's for the same cause—in the latter case falsely called remorse by prejudiced biographers. Or family ties may be of such strength, as with the Brontë sisters, that from their dissolution there is no return to happiness. Nature may become part of the artist's self—the Lakes with Wordsworth, the moors with the Brontës, the mountains with Rousseau, the forests of the New World with Chateaubriand. Emily Brontë nearly died of homesickness when separated from her beloved scene.

The artist must have the last word, because his career, though often self-destructive, points to a higher truth and, ultimately, a more certain faith. Granted the sacredness of the fact, granted that life consists in adjusting the movements of the mind to the outer world and extracting its divine meaning, yet the artist makes us aware of a finer set of

[1] *History of Criticism*, Vol. I, p. 314, note.

facts, the rhythm of which with our earthly life he is in process of discovering. Once in the world a great man arose who described worthily the events in which he had played a part, namely, Thucydides and the Peloponnesian War; but it was said of the American Stephen Crane that he wrote better about war in his novels before he had seen it, than afterwards, as newspaper correspondent, when he had seen it. The test of a mind's quality is the distance it can travel from the fact and yet remain true to itself.[1] Chekhov defined culture as that which makes the heart ache for what the eye does not see. Humour is a quality of the finest minds and most advanced civilizations, and it is finer and truer in proportion as its relations with factual reality are most unorthodox. The Philistine is harmless at his work, when he is ballasted by the fact, but the reverse of harmless at his play or in his jokes. Goethe said that action was easy, thought hard; and Plato defined the philosopher as the spectator of all time and all existence. Thinkers from Pythagoras, Plato, and Aristotle down the ages to Dr. Arnold Toynbee have emphasized that contemplation is the noblest form of activity.[2] The list includes Dante who, in the *Convivio* (III, 11), dissociates the true philosopher from applied wisdom. Dante's paraphrase of the Lord's Prayer has beauty distinct from its sacred original. Lines that are literal translations such as,

'Do oggi a noi la cotidiana manna',[3]

are stamped with his seal, because beauty is an ultimate, an experience that speaks for itself and requires no proof, and so we feel that his prayer is answered and has become a fact

[1] 'The mind of a human being increasingly organizes itself apart from the processes which control the body' (W. Temple, *op. cit.*, p. 467).

[2] Bergson, however, contrasts the incomplete Greek and Indian mysticism, which stays at contemplation, with the true Christian mysticism which issues in action (*op. cit.*, pp. 234–248).

[3] 'Give us this day our daily bread' (*Purgatorio*, XI. 1–21).

in the universe. As the artist discovers more and more correspondence between those furthest thoughts and our present needs, he will achieve not only a week-day but a Sabbath faith, and restore art to her true office of religion's handmaid.[1] And he will be received again into men's councils, because his gift to them is relief from the sadness which fills the mind when its thoughts range far into the future. To him it will be conceded that the reality he touches is truer than that of law or politics or business; and in return he will accept material responsibility, and so, by interacting more fully with his environment, stand in the presence of God. That the lure of art is of all others the most irresistible is proved by the fact that no true artist, except Arthur Rimbaud, has ever deliberately abandoned art. 'The beautiful is something ultimate which cannot be resolved into anything else'[2]; and the artist therefore pursues no will-o'-the-wisp, but seeks for a correspondence that exists somewhere between earth and heaven. The quarrel has long divided mankind, for Plato, though he loved Homer, banished him and all poets from the ideal State, because the poet is thrice removed from reality[3]; while the Arabs kindled bonfires when a poet appeared among them. The best argument for the truth of the mystic experience is that its effect 'is not exhaustion but enhancement of life and power and added strength'.[4]

The devout Elizabethans, if they wished to achieve an object, first prayed to God, and then gave God a chance of answering their prayers by doing all that lay in their own power to bring it about. We thus continually return to our

[1] 'The potential being of man extends beyond the world, and man must therefore seek to meet God in God's own quiet beyond the world' (Edwyn Bevan, *op. cit.*, p. 124).

[2] *Ibid.*, p. 143.

[3] *Republic*, X.

[4] T. H. Hughes, *The Philosophic Basis of Mysticism*, pp. 215–16. Cf. Radhakrishnan, 'The normal mystic has a burning passion for social righteousness' (*op. cit.*, p. 109).

starting point that mastery of the seen world is the needful approach to the unseen. And yet of all the promises in the Gospel there is surely none more encouraging than this: 'I say unto you, Though he will not rise and give him because he is his friend, yet because of his importunity he will rise and give him as many as he needeth. And I say unto you, Ask, and it shall be given you; seek, and ye shall find; knock, and it shall be opened unto you. For every one that asketh receiveth; and he that seeketh findeth; and to him that knocketh it shall be opened.'[1] It was Dante's habit to interweave Scriptural and classical quotations, and we will therefore conclude with his strains in our ears:

> 'Vegna ver noi la pace del tuo regno,
> Che noi ad essa non potem da noi,
> S'ella non vien, con tutto nostro ingegno.'[2]

[1] Luke xi.

[2] *Purgatorio*, XI. 7–9: 'Grant us the peace of Thy Kingdom, which, if it come not, we ourselves cannot gain, with all our understanding.'

POETRY AND FAITH

POETRY AND FAITH

Man is most himself when co-operating with God, and his highest state is communion with God. Newman said that before accepting the Roman Catholic faith he was convinced that there need be nothing between his soul and God, not even the Virgin Mary. In his greatest moments man withdraws from the world, and he requires periods of solitude in which to develop his final powers. Human nature is at its worst in crowds, and improves as the ways of life's pilgrimage are more and more thinly populated. Discipline must needs be stricter as the numbers that make up a group are larger, beginning with the army, and ending with the school, or even the family; and the best conversation is between two persons only: hence the transforming effect of love, and the saying that all true lovers are friends besides. A confidence shared between two is sacred, but if we discover that our friend has confided the same thing to half a dozen others, the light of common day intrudes. The more openly a subject is discussed, the greater the number of minds through which it passes, the more it loses its mystery and becomes vulgarized. There is an illness with which human beings infect each other but from which they are immune in solitude, and Hazlitt was right to say that vulgarity was conventional, not natural, coarseness. As man progresses, he must free himself from all relationships, beginning with the crowd, and ending even with himself, with all useless self-questioning and internal babbling—since Plato declared thinking itself to be a dialogue within the soul. Next to the prophet it is the poet who takes us furthest along this road to silence and co-operation with God.

A few examples of the poet's art will set us on the way. We will take Byron's well-known lines on the dying gladiator:

'He recked not of the life he lost or prize,
But where his rude hut by the Danube lay,
There were his young barbarians all at play,
There was their Dacian mother, he their sire
Butchered to make a Roman holiday. . . .'

Byron was a rhetorician nine times out of ten, and there is more rhetoric than poetry here. He speaks like an orator, conscious of an audience, to whom he gives and from whom he receives, becoming more effective as their emotion waxes, and the greater the audience the greater the emotion. The same may be said of Mark Antony's oration in *Julius Caesar* (in which the disintegrators suspect the hand of Marlowe), even in this climactic passage:

'For when the noble Caesar saw him stab,
Ingratitude more strong than traitors' arms
Quite vanquished him; then burst his mighty heart. . . .'

But when we read some lines previously,

'But yesterday the word of Caesar might
Have stood against the world, now lies he there
And none so poor to do him reverence. . . .'

we discover a different quality, and are nearer to the line if we do not quite pass it. Now let us consider a passage in Belial's speech in the second book of *Paradise Lost*:

'What if the breath that kindled those grim fires
Awaked should blow them into sevenfold rage
And plunge us in the flames, or from above
Should intermitted vengeance arm again
His red right hand to plague us; what if all
Her stores were opened and this firmament
Of hell should spout her cataracts of fire. . . .'

This also is rhetorical because the situation requires rhetoric, yet in the intervals between the voices of the thunder we touch the land of silence. The old saying that lyric poetry should not be heard but overheard is true of all poetry; and the greatest poet takes us furthest into that silent hemisphere which is the antipodes of our noisy one. Let us, then, stand at the gate of the temple which is called Beautiful, resolved that what enters our souls in the silent intervals amid his music is the poet's truth.

I

HOMER

It is often said that ancient poetry excels in form, modern poetry in imagination: and, like all popular sayings, this is made up of truth and error, because imagination is the soul of poetry, and no poetry without it would be worth the name. That it has some meaning we shall see if we compare the following lines by Homer and Shakespeare. When Shakespeare writes,

> 'That time of year thou may'st in me behold
> When yellow leaves, or none, or few, do hang
> Upon those boughs which shake against the cold . . .'[1]

he is thinking of no particular trees but of the spirit of autumn and its significance for human life. But when we read in the *Iliad*,

> 'ὣς δ'ὅτ ἄν ἐκ πόντοιο σέλας ναύτῃσι φανήῃ
> καιομένοιο πυρός· τό δε καίεται ὑψόθ' ὄρεσφι
> σταθμῷ ἐν οἰοπόλῳ . . .'[2]

we feel that this is a sight actually seen on a Greek island that could be named. It would seem, therefore, as if Shakespeare expressed the ideal and Homer the real, but this is not so. Both are equally ideal, and it is not so much the beauty of the language and the music of the verse that defeat the translator, as that 'ethereal and fifth essence' which is the breath of poetry itself—as Milton called it, the breath of reason.[3]

[1] Sonnet LXXIII.

[2] XIX. 375–7: 'As when over the sea there appears to sailors the gleam of a fire, burning high among the mountains in a lonely farmstead.'

[3] *Areopagitica*.

To express this fifth essence is the duty of the poet; to experience it, that of the critic; and if he can describe his emotion adequately, he is more likely to win disciples for his master than the translator. Many are the translators of Homer, but by none is his spirit captured, least of all by the 'clarion couplets' of Pope, as Frederic Harrison described them.[1] There is another way of approach for the Greekless reader, and that is through the original works of scholar-poets such as Milton and Gray; but these again are powerless before Homer. Milton's blank verse, according to Matthew Arnold, is 'self-retarding', and this is the opposite to Homer's rapidity, to that 'slide' of his verse which, as Bacon said, eclipsed all other. Myers defined poetry as the fusion of thought and melody: for it is neither the meaning of the words alone nor their sound alone that creates a poem. When a singer pauses in his song but the accompanying music continues, the effect is sometimes more beautiful than when the voice is sounding, and in that moment of reverie we learn even more about the voice's true quality. So, while reading poetry, it is the echoes as they prolong themselves in our minds that bring us into contact with the essential poet: as Wordsworth retained in his heart the music of the Highland reaper long after he had passed beyond the range of her voice. If, therefore, it could be possible to match these overtones in a foreign language, we might get a Sinai-like vision of the God Homer.

In all the English poetry known to me there is only one passage that reminds me of Homer. The comparison may be less just than that of Dr. Mackail's between Pindar and Meredith,[2] and may excite ridicule or even anger, but nevertheless I will make it. It is to a poet whose kingly crown

[1] Certain passages in the Waverley novels are nearer to the Homeric spirit than the translations: e.g., the storming of the castle in *Ivanhoe*, and the deeds of the Black Knight with his thundering axe; also the rekindling of the beacon in *Peveril* (Vol. II, Ch. IX).

[2] *Lectures on Greek Poetry* (1910), pp. 118–19.

among the greater singers has long been forfeit, yet who is still the friend of uncritical youth—namely, Byron. Let us dwell upon the echoes of these lines, describing a sunset in Greece, before they fade from the mind:

> 'On old Aegina's rock and Idra's isle
> The god of gladness sheds his parting smile. . . .
> Descending fast the mountain shadows kiss
> Thy glorious gulf, unconquered Salamis! . . .
> On such an eve his palest beam he cast,
> When, Athens! here thy Wisest looked his last. . . .' [1]

Now consider these two short passages from the *Iliad*, the first of which refers to one of the designs on the shield of Achilles:

> 'ἡ δὲ μελαίνετ' ὄπισθεν, ἀρηρομένῃ δε ἐῴκει
> χρυσείη περ ἐοῦσα· τὸ δὴ περὶ θαῦμα τέτυκτο' [2]
> . . . .
> ' . . . εἰς ὅ κεν ἔλθῃ
> δείελος ὀψὲ δύων, σκιάσῃ δ' ἐρίβωλον ἄρουραν.' [3]

In both poets the emotion is produced by the earth, by its great age, and the thought of the generations that have arisen and departed and performed great actions.

This emotion of the earth may serve as an introduction to Homer's quality. He is as much concerned with active, pulsing life as Shakespeare, and with the struggle of opposing characters, yet he is remote from the world. Dr. Mackail has said that Greek poetry, after the time of Homer and Sappho, achieved its triumphs 'through minds overburdened with thought' [4]; and as no one can refuse to Homer the power of deep thought, the difference must lie in the nature of the thought. Homer has made the story of the Trojan war and

[1] *Corsair*, Canto III.

[2] XVIII. 548–9: 'And the field grew black behind, as if it were being ploughed, although it was gold, and this was the great wonder'.

[3] XXI. 231–2: 'Until late-coming evening overshadow the deep-soiled earth'.

[4] *Op. cit.*, p. 113.

the personalities of its heroes his own in a way that no other poet or writer in the world has ever approached, so that when others have treated it, we are conscious of a lack, of a feeling of homesickness as for a vanished age of beauty. I refer to the Greek tragedians, even to Aeschylus, and above all to Euripides, whose plays are populated with Homeric characters, and the reading of whose *Trojan Women* makes one conscious of a continued ache or regret to see the divine light of the master yielding to the light of common day. It is needless to compare Virgil's Andromache with the original[1]; and comparisons with Shakespeare's *Troilus and Cressida* or Chaucer's *Troilus and Criseyde* would be inappropriate. The nearest approach to such a monopoly—though on a lower level—is Boswell's biography of Johnson, though we grant that the meeting with Dr. Johnson in Thackeray's *Virginians* is very pleasant. Such a lack would not be felt were we to read the story of creation by another poet than Milton.

Homer was not overburdened by the kind of thought that develops from the strife of human minds with each other. Even the highest philosophy—such as Plato's, except in the myths—is an argument, a constant interplay of mind with mind[2]; but Homer is like the mystic to whom the vision has been revealed in solitude, and who then returns to earth to do his work and help his fellow creatures; and because of his experience, though he is in the world he is not of it. Argument is noisy, and when we read the *Trojan Women* we are conscious of a babble of voices, of many earthly veils between the poet's soul and God; but when we read Homer we feel in ourselves a deep silence through all the clash of arms. The depth of this silence is the measure of a poet's greatness: the extent to which we feel, as we surrender ourselves to the waking trance, that there is no god but God, and the poet is His prophet. There are mystery silences in Aeschylus, less deep than Homer but deeper than Sophocles, and those in

[1] *Aeneid*, III.

[2] Plato defined thinking as the soul's dialogue with itself.

Euripides are slight by comparison, except in the *Bacchae* and portions of the *Iphigenia in Aulis*. One reason why Shakespeare's *Antony and Cleopatra* is below the four great tragedies is that there are no soliloquies where Antony communes with his inner self and we see him alone with the universe.

Given these silences in which we are alone with Homer, what is it about him that touches us so nearly, and makes his verse as fresh as when it was first spoken nearly three thousand years ago? His world is not our world, and his battles certainly not ours, now that war is mechanized and men no longer use spear and shield. Yet he communicates to us his delight in the fine armour of his warriors, especially in the new arms forged for Achilles. On two occasions the spears aimed at Achilles pierce the four outer folds, of tin and bronze, of his shield, but are stayed by the gold—and the gold fascinates us with its beauty.[1] We are like children absorbed in a fairy story—only let this be taken literally, not in the sense that we are grown-up children. The emotion of children is more powerful because they believe that the fairy world is real. We are apt to think of fairy tales as strange and fantastic, written merely to amuse; but they go far deeper. No child can feel the same after reading Grimm's stories, for a new world is suddenly revealed as part of his own, and corroborated by the fears and anxieties that have lurked inarticulate in his mind. His elders cannot protect him, for the laws that govern the usual world no longer hold. At any moment the walls may part asunder to admit the passage of a dwarf; or a benevolent-looking stranger may call at the house and suddenly change to a winged djin and carry him off. In Goethe's poem the child, riding with his father through the forest, is accosted by the Erl-King, whom he points out to his father:

'"Oh, 'tis the Erl-King with his crown and his shroud."
"No, my son, it is but a dark wreath of the cloud."'

[1] XX. 268; XXI. 165.

The Erl-King tries to entice the child away to be his daughter's playmate:

'"O father, my father, and saw you not plain
The Erl-King's pale daughter glide past thro' the rain?"
"Oh yes, my loved treasure, I knew it full soon;
It was the grey willow that danced to the moon."'

The Erl-King becomes impatient and threatens to drag him away:

'"The Erl-King has seized me—his grasp is so cold!"'

'Sore trembled the father; he spurred thro' the wild,
Clasping close to his bosom his shuddering child;
He reaches his dwelling in doubt and in dread,
But, clasp'd to his bosom, the infant was dead.'[1]

Homer touches this region of mystery, this sense of a world other than our own, which we know to be real, as the child responds to the reality of the fairy tale. He lived before the Orphic or other mystery religions were known in Greece: his religion was of the cheerful kind, free from superstition or fear of the ghost-world, and he troubled little about life after death.[2] Yet we stand in his presence with the same awe as we feel for theological poets like Aeschylus and Dante. By no translators are we so misled as by those modern colloquial ones who make Nausicaa address King Alcinous as 'Daddy'; or those critics who call the *Odyssey* the first European novel. There are enough homely details in the Old Testament, yet the twenty-fourth chapter of Genesis, where they abound, is unequalled for sublimity. Homer never declines from sublimity, and we therefore ask what this world is that touches us so nearly, like the fairy world but without its terror—what the nature is of the awe that we feel, like religious awe, but not directly religious. The answer is that in the silences that

[1] Walter Scott's translation.

[2] See article, *Greek Religion*, in 14th edition of *Encyclopædia Britannica*.

occur amid his music we realize that the poet has seen God, and is revealing to us not rules of behaviour or examples of good and evil but, like Shakespeare, something of the joy of God in His creation.

We will now recall the devices which Homer uses to convey his message. Achilles, greatest of the Greek warriors, has withdrawn from the battle because Agamemnon has treated him unfairly. For two-thirds of the story we are entertained by the deeds of great men, but less great than Achilles. We delight in the prowess of Agamemnon, the two Ajax's, Diomed, Menelaus, Odysseus—and, on the Trojan side, Hector, Aeneas, Sarpedon, and others. They are great enough, and skilled with spear and sword, and we are dazzled by the gleam of the bronze of their corslets and shields and greaves; yet we long to see Achilles using these same things with greater effect. You would think the might of a warrior could be no further told when Ajax bestrides the body of Patroclus and covers it with his shield that is like the wall of a city,[1] yet Homer surpasses it by adding to Achilles speed and beauty. When the Greeks are hard pressed and their ships nearly burnt, Patroclus begs Achilles to let him join the fight. Achilles consents, and equips Patroclus in his armour, only withholding the spear which no one but he can wield. Patroclus is slain by Hector and despoiled; and now Achilles will fight to avenge his friend, but he has no armour. While the new armour is forging, he stands beside the trench and shouts at the advancing Trojans: and the mere sight of him confounds them. Then, resplendent in his new arms, blazing like the sun, he mounts his chariot and is borne into battle by the divine coursers.

But despite the glorious apparition of Achilles in arms, and the beam of his shield that strikes the skies, he is not based upon externals, as it has been said of Scott's heroes, especially Claverhouse with his plumes and jack-boots. It is his own vital spark that irradiates these outer things and

[1] *Iliad*, XVII. 128 ff.

extends even to nature. In one of the grandest of all passages —the struggle with the river—the god raises a huge wave, with darkness on its crest, to overwhelm him, and sends down a torrent with roaring of stones and tree-stumps. After his angry passage with Apollo who had decoyed him from the battle, he speeds across the plain towards Troy; and, to Priam, who watches from the city, the bronze of his corslet blazes like the evil-boding star of autumn, or the rising sun. In the final onset against Hector the light from his spear-point flashes forth like Hesperus in the darkness, fairest of the stars in heaven. All these images are beautiful because of the man; they receive as much as they give. It is the beauty of the human form in action that Homer celebrates, as part of God's scheme of the world. Therefore we consent in our inner minds to the victory of Achilles over Hector, because, though Hector is more sympathetic, the measure of his divine strength and energy is heaped with a less generous hand. The word 'divine' should be taken literally, to avoid any suggestion of brute force or Nietzsche's superman. It is the gift of God for a purpose that we do not know, beyond ordinary good and evil. Our minds are entranced by the beauty of the verse, and we believe the Homeric world to be real, as children believe in a fairy world that is other than the usual world, yet touches them nearly.

There is dramatic meaning in the moral superiority of Hector; he becomes thereby a worthier adversary of Achilles. The strength and skill of Achilles are heightened by the quality of the being whom he overthrows. Other writers of epics and romances promise great events in the future, but their power is often spent in anticipation, and the fulfilment is disappointing. Only Homer is great in preparation and greater in climax; the thunder of his verse out-echoes itself in the final shock of the two champions. We do not really regret the fall of the chivalrous Hector; and yet Monro dwelt much on the sadness of the *Iliad*. There is sadness in the main theme, in the destiny of man, but joy in the floodlight of the imagination. War is cruel to youth, and there are many who die far from home, like Hippothous, and never reward beloved parents for the care of upbringing.[1] Hector is the loser in a game of which we do not know the rules, but we are charmed by Homer and accept his interpretation of the will of God. Compare with him a poet only one degree less great but whose mind was 'overburdened by thought' —Aeschylus. When Clytemnestra speaks of the 'much-wept Iphigenia',[2] we feel the stab of human grief, we are conscious of what Pater called 'the great stream of human tears falling always through the shadows of the world'. Fate is mightier even than Zeus, but in Aeschylus we think more of what man has made of man; there is still a gap between poet and philosopher. In Homer sorrow is part of the heavenly pattern; we receive it more easily into our minds, reconcile it with truth through beauty. The silence is not broken by voices pleading for justice in earthly courts. And because Homer with his music is our mediator, we believe him when he tells us that the beauty of the perfectly trained human form in action is part of God's intention. As surety for the reality of Achilles, he wraps him in the starry mantle of the heavens, and crowns him with the fiery signs that burn in the sky at harvest time, and carves his pillar of fame highest in the minds of men through their fear and wonder. Nor is there lacking in the spectrum the more sober colour of early death chosen as the price of glory, rather than obscure old age: of which we are often reminded, but never more impressively than when the horse Xanthus is suddenly given speech[3] and foretells to Achilles his doom in lines that fall like shooting stars from the heaven of poetry.

It is probably true that the great passages of the *Iliad* are the summit of the world's poetry, but in charm the *Odyssey* surpasses the *Iliad*. There are glimpses of finer things, haunts of peace and immortal love, removed from the brawl-

[1] XVII. 300–2. [2] *Agamemnon* 1526.

[3] XIX. 404 ff.

ing world. The outer framework is action—the wanderings and shipwrecks of Odysseus, his adventures with the Cyclops and other monsters, the passage between Scylla and Charybdis, the final slaying of the wooers—but at the heart is a golden calm. It is like the shadowy hills of the isle of Scheria that rise on the vision of Odysseus as he draws near in his raft, and appear like a shield in the misty deep[1]; or like Shelley's island in *Epipsychidion* lying in an azure chasm of calm left by thunderstorms that pass over to other lands. Man must still fight to keep his place in the world, but he no longer fights for the joy of fighting. He looks forward to the time when the battle shall be over, and he can be at ease in his home and converse with his wife and friends and former comrades in action.

Ancient poetry is said to deal with outward things and modern with inward, but all true poetry, in its last analysis, is inward. The pain of bereavement has never been expressed more poignantly than in these concluding lines of the speech of the shade of Anticleia, mother of Odysseus, in the lower world:

> ‘ἀλλά με σός τε πόθος σά τε μήδεα φαίδιμ’ Ὀδυσσεῦ
> σή τ’ ἀγανοφροσύνη μελιηδέα θυμὸν ἀπηύρα.’[2]

The prizes of life must be fought for and, when gained, valiantly defended, but there is an overplus of thought. There is a region of the mind where man walks with God. Circe will not detain Odysseus against his will,[3] and Calypso speaks these immortal lines:

> ‘καὶ γὰρ ἐμοὶ νόος ἐστὶν ἐναίσιμος, οὐδέ μοι αὐτῇ
> θυμὸς ἐνὶ στήθεσσι σιδήρεος, ἀλλ’ ἐλεήμων.’[4]

[1] V. 281–2.

[2] XI. 202–3: ‘It was desire for thee and thy counsels, O noble Odysseus, and thy loving-kindness, that bereft me of sweet life.’

[3] X. 489.

[4] V. 190–1: ‘For I also have a righteous mind, and my heart within me is not of iron, but pitiful.’

It is not fear for themselves that makes Odysseus and those of his company who remain weep for their comrades who are subdued by Circe's spell, but homesickness for lost friends, for the breaking of mystical human ties. When the spell is reversed, they appear younger than before their transformation, goodlier and taller.[1] Calypso, in lines of equal beauty to those already quoted, laments the command of Zeus to release Odysseus:

> 'τὸν μὲν ἐγὼ φιλεόν τε καὶ ἔτρεφον, ἠδὲ ἔφασκον
> θήσειν ἀθάνατον καὶ ἀγήρων ἤματα πάντα.'[2]

The actions of the *Iliad* are clear-cut and performed in the sunlight, those of the *Odyssey* are shadowed by the emotions of men. The speech of the characters in the *Iliad* is one with action; in the *Odyssey* there is an interval of meditation, of memory of the past, of hope or fear for the future. It means something that Odysseus, though divinely protected, is troubled in spirit when he goes alone to the house of Circe,[3] and that his heart is broken by the tidings that he must visit the realm of Hades.[4] He often alludes to his 'dear company', and though Elpenor was neither brave in battle nor steadfast in mind,[5] his comrades lament his death and shed tears at his funeral pyre. There are degrees of friendship, and Odysseus speaks of Polites as the dearest and most trusted of his company.[6] There is even excess of weeping for the lost ones, the grief of those who will not be comforted,[7] who remember the past and are anxious for the future, who do not live the purely outward lives that the ancient Greeks were said to live. Every adventure takes its toll of victims and thins the ranks, until those who remain are swallowed up in the deep gulfs of the sea, and only Odysseus survives to tell the tale. The fate of these men is piteous because of the breaking of the bond of

[1] X. 395–6.

[2] V. 135–6: 'Him have I loved and cherished, and I said I would make him to be immortal and grow not old.'

[3] X. 309. [4] X. 496. [5] X. 552–3. [6] X. 224–5.

[7] X. 198–202.

love—a love which becomes poignant at the approach of danger. It is an ideal which belongs to the world of Homer, and makes our own world poorer for its lack. Odysseus, in the end, returns to his home and wife and friends, and to a peaceful old age, but he will not forget his sorrow, in the words of Zophar the Naamathite, or remember it as waters that pass away. Achilles mourns for Patroclus, and Andromache regrets that Hector spoke no last word that she might keep in her mind day and night,[1] but, could the dead awaken, we feel they would resume their lives as before. The *Odyssey* has another story—of sorrow remembered in joy, sorrow that interacts with joy, sorrow that becomes music in the voice of Odysseus when, safe in that finer world where the stranger-suppliant is dear as a brother, he tells of the storm without.

The Homeric Greeks were described by Jebb as refined and open-handed. The Homeric Zeus was a god of mercy who would assuredly punish those who disregarded the prayers of the afflicted or turned the suppliant from their doors. King Alcinous gives the wanderer Odysseus a royal welcome, hears his story in spellbound silence, and sends him on his way with costly gifts. The earlier adventures of Odysseus gain in interest because they are told, in present security, to friendly listeners. The presence of the faithful wife Penelope is felt throughout the whole poem, and so is the yearning of Odysseus for his home. Nothing in all his wanderings caused Odysseus such agony as the loss of those of his men whom Scylla devoured, who called upon him by name for the last time.[2] The spirits in the lower world stand sorrowing round Odysseus, and question him of those they loved on earth.[3] Agamemnon relates with incurable grief the story of his wife's treachery.[4] Achilles would rather live as a hireling on earth than rule among the dead.[5] Earth and heaven meet in Nausicaa, who was like to the gods in form

[1] *Iliad*, XXIV. 744–5. [2] XII. 245–59. [3] XI. 541–2. [4] XI. 404–34. [5] XI. 488–91.

and comeliness, and attended by handmaids dowered with beauty from the Graces.[1] Odysseus could hold his own in the strife of minds, even if a god opposed him.[2] God is present in all human relations, from the friendship of comrades in danger, suddenly made conscious by death or absence, refined as it spreads upwards through every state of life, till it touches kings and queens in their withdrawn splendour. The immortals know each other, even though they live far away, as when Hermes and Calypso meet.[3]

The gods of ancient Greece differed in degree but not in kind from human beings; they were stronger, wiser, more beautiful, and also exempt from the sorrow which is the lot of man.[4] Zeus describes man as the most wretched thing on earth, and when he sees the divine horses in the midst of the battle weeping for the fall of Patroclus, with downcast heads and manes trailing in the dust, he half regrets that he gave them to Peleus, if, themselves immortal, they are to share in the sorrows of mortals.[5] In the *Iliad* it is strength and speed that make Achilles godlike; in the *Odyssey* the softer traits prevail. Not only the command of Zeus but something in herself urges Calypso to set free Odysseus; and Circe is touched with pity when her spell is broken. Alcinous receives kindly the shipwrecked Odysseus, and bestows gifts upon him and the promise of a convoy; the queen Arete makes her gracious presence felt, though she speaks little; the maiden Nausicaa glows with beauty, and is wise in speech beyond her years: and by these paths we enter the courts of heaven. Spontaneous kindness, unsuspecting belief in the stranger, suggest that this is the true life, the true home, the heaven where we are meant to dwell—that this place of men's strivings and corrupt practices and cruelty to each other is the illusion. As sea and sky mingle at dawn or sunset, and unearthly light flows over the edge of the world, so, moving through dazzling words, we feel the divine inter-

[1] VI. 16–18. [2] XIII. 291–2. [3] V. 79–80.
[4] *Iliad*, XXIV. 525–6. [5] *Iliad*, XVII. 443–7.

penetrate the human, and converse equally with men or gods. The last impression—and in this Homer approaches Dante—is that when man is at rest, his enemies scattered, his surroundings beautiful, he can receive something from a higher soul that passes the love of women. If the *Iliad* is the apotheosis of manhood, the *Odyssey* grants us a vision of a state that we share with God. There is a hint of constancy in affection that is part of the music of the spheres and will inform the life of all men when battles are over and seas are stilled.

In the *Iliad* men actually fight with gods: Diomed even wounded Ares, the god of war, and sent him bellowing with pain out of the battle[1]; and Achilles scolded Apollo.[2] The *Odyssey* tells of a subtle relation between gods and men, of a peace that gods can confer on favoured mortals. The greatest innovation of the Hebrew religion was its teaching the love, as well as the fear, of God—of a God who walked with Adam in the Garden of Eden, not a hostile God who needed constantly to be propitiated by sacrifice. There is an eternal charm in those stories which tell how men have unawares entertained angels. Such is the old Greek story of Apollo and Admetus king of Pherae in Thessaly, beautifully retold by William Morris in the *Earthly Paradise*: how the disguised Apollo sojourned with Admetus and brought blessings to his house, and when he departed something of his spirit remained, so that wars ceased, and harvests were bountiful, and the golden age returned to Pherae. The *Odyssey* does not suggest a golden age that has vanished but something that the poet has recreated for us, something in which we share by the might and quality of his inspiration. Swords may clash and arrows fly, and snares be set for the unwary, but there is a greater reality than strife: and that is the effect of mind on mind which can make man equal to the gods. Homer protracts this emotion throughout the *Odyssey*—the question in the eyes of those who have seen God revealed in man, and hope for further knowledge as

[1] *Iliad*, V. 855–63. [2] *Iliad*, XXII. 15–20.

they gaze on a fellow mortal. Odysseus is still the native of a world where he must toil and suffer, but intersecting it is another world, into which he can exchange at times, where he emulates the peace, the beauty, the conversation of the gods. This magic light informs the *Odyssey* like the Soul, or atom of the Eternal, which burnt in the heart of Shelley's island, felt but not seen, and filled the interstices of rocks and forests.

I think Myers went too far when he said that beside Homer's speech Virgil's seems elaborate, and Dante's crabbed, and Shakespeare's barbarous; but it is true that Homer delights the soul like no other poet, and the reason is that he does not select and reject but transmutes the whole of life into poetry, so that we gain both the world and our own souls, and he shows such as have eyes to see that the strength of men, the beauty of women, the loyalty of friends, the joys of social intercourse, the yearning for home, the kindness of earth's great ones to the suppliant—all these things proceed directly from God.

II

VIRGIL AND HORACE

Sainte-Beuve divided poets into two classes—those who, like nature, produced a mountain with its grandeur and also its barrenness, and those who built a palace and made it perfect by the touch of human hands. Virgil is of the latter, and some windows of his palace are shuttered and curtained, while others reflect the rising and setting suns. The true Virgil is modern and inward, and the memory of these passages persists amid the outer events which he describes, and exalts the whole poem. It has been said that he aimed in the *Georgics* to reawaken in the heart of the people the love of agriculture, fallen into decay during the civil wars that had devastated the country; and to make of the *Aeneid* a national poem glorifying the newly founded Empire[1]; but poetry is beyond teaching, and we must look for Virgil himself not in his formal design but his last echoes.

Two of the finest modern critics, Myers and Mackail, have surpassed themselves in writing about Virgil. 'Infinite pity' is Dr. Mackail's last word on the subject, and he quotes Newman's saying that in Virgil we hear 'the voice of Nature herself'. The suggestive power of the greatest literature, however, is inexhaustible, and it may be possible to carry the enquiry one step further by observing the circumstances in which this faculty operates. It is agreed, I think, that Virgil's genius culminates in the sixth book of the *Aeneid*, and if we examine the cause for this preference, and find passages in other books that suggest the same emotion, a further truth may emerge. We get the key to it in the most famous of his

[1] J. W. Mackail.

lines, about 'the tears of things' and 'mortal affairs that touch the heart'.[1] The occasion is when Aeneas discovers in the new-built temple at Carthage the Trojan scenes worked by artists on the walls, and knows that the story of his sorrows and those of his race has penetrated to the world's confines. He does not brood over these thoughts in silence but imparts them to the loyal Achates. This emotion again assails us in the speech of the ghost of Creusa, the wife of Aeneas, when she appears to him on the night of the sack of Troy, and tells that she is lost to him for ever—above all, in this line:

'Longa tibi exsilia et vastum maris aequor arandum.'[2]

And another instance is the speech of the Sea-Nymphs, into which the ships of Aeneas have been transformed, when they swim round him and encourage him to continue his course:

'Nos sumus Idaeae sacro de vertice pinus,
Nunc pelagi nymphae, classis tua.'[3]

In all these it is less the thing itself that moves us than the speech about it, or rather the extra meaning that the thing acquires by its transmission from mind to mind.

I have already remarked on the regret we feel for Homer when any subject he has treated reappears in another poet. We experience this to the full in reading the *Aeneid*, where so much is reflected Homer—namely the sea-adventures of the early books, the funeral games of Book V, and the battles of the last books; so that we must look beyond the formal plan to discover the true Virgil. The fourth book—the episode of Dido—is the most popular, and, in a sense, the most dramatic, but this is not unqualified praise, since Virgil's genius was not essentially dramatic. The reality of Dido's passion is beyond doubt, but the soul of Aeneas is in shadow,

1 I. 462.

2 II. 780: 'A far-off exile is your fate, and vast expanse of sea to plough.'

3 X. 230–1: 'We are the pines cut from the holy crest of Ida, now Nymphs of the sea, once your fleet.'

and no gleam of fire breaks through. Despite his modern apologists,[1] we recall Dryden's saying that the Thracian Maenads would have served him for his lack of constancy in the same way as they served Orpheus for excessive constancy. It may be true that he was vowed to a greater quest than love, but in Shakespeare's hands the struggle would not have appeared one-sided. When Shakespeare portrayed Shylock he intended to make him odious, because of the prevailing anti-Jewish sentiment, but he was borne on by the impetus of his dramatic genius to make him human. If, therefore, Book IV is a triumph, it is one rather of ingenuity, since all Virgil's poetic forces are not engaged.

These may be said to be concentrated in Book VI, where Aeneas visits the underworld. Virgil excels in retrospective, not direct, narrative, in depicting human beings stricken in mind by the effect of past misfortunes. Foremost of his pictures are the crowds of unburied dead beseeching Charon, with outstretched arms, to convey them in his boat across the Styx. We hear the pilot Palinurus, still loyal at heart to Aeneas, tell how he was attacked and left to drown by the inhabitants of the Italian coast. Dido, wandering in the Mourning Fields, uncertain as the moon through cloud, is more pathetic than in her rage or even her suicide. His former comrades in arms gather wistfully round Aeneas and keep step with him as he walks. It is not often that Latin excels Greek, but it does so here, when this line from Homer,

'νήγρετος ἥδιστος, θανάτῳ ἄγχιστα ἐοικώς',[2]

recurs, literally translated, in the speech of Deiphobus:

'Dulcis et alta quies placidaeque simillima morti'[3].

We get the long roll of heroes whose deeds will establish

[1] See T. R. Glover, *Studies in Virgil* (1904), pp. 202–4.

[2] *Odyssey*, XIII. 80: 'A deep and sweet sleep, the nearest thing to death'.

[3] *Aeneid*, VI. 522.

Rome above all nations. Their brows are shaded with wreaths of civic oak, he tells us in one of his greatest lines:

> 'Atque umbrata gerunt civili tempora quercu'.[1]

Apart from the two great episodes, nothing moves us like the passage on the young Marcellus. The words 'Purpureos spargam flores'[2] touch the quick of beauty as nearly as any music of speech can do.

The first of the episodes in which the poem culminates is the description of the Elysian Fields. If the concluding lines (660–5) are compared with those of a later speech of Anchises (847–53), we shall learn something of Virgil's true quality. The first are more visionary, the second more exact. In the one we glimpse a world of self-sacrificing patriots, of pious servants of truth and religion, of inventors of beautiful things; the other presents a well-ordered, well-governed world, such as Rome was to become, based on fact as well as imagination. In the first there is a remote, homeless quality that belongs to Virgil at his best—that same quality which W. P. Ker found in the finest medieval poems; and if we pass on to the greatest passage of all in the *Aeneid*—the meeting with Anchises—we learn still more. As Aeneas approaches, Anchises, with bursts of tears and outstretched arms, begins,

> 'Venisti tandem, tuaque expectata parenti
> Vicit iter durum pietas?'[3]

and the surge of emotion, animating every line of his speech and enduring to the last word, is renewed in Aeneas, and carries him to a yet greater height:

> '... Tua me, genitor, tua tristis imago
> Saepius occurrens haec limina tendere adegit....'[4]

Anchises speaks of vast expanses of land and sea that Aeneas

[1] *Ibid.* 772. [2] *Ibid.* 884: 'I scatter brilliant flowers'.

[3] *Ibid.* 687–8: 'Hast thou come at last, and has the piety which thy father looked for overcome the hard way?'

[4] *Ibid.* 695–6: 'Father, thy sad phantom, often appearing, forced me to seek this haven.'

has traversed on his way, and we remember the prophecy of Creusa. As a complement to these, we may cite this line spoken by the Sibyl,

> '. . . illius ergo
> Venimus et magnos Erebi tranavimus amnis',[1]

to be confirmed in our opinion that there is an extra pressure of Virgil's soul on lines that describe movement: and independence of time and space is one of the soul's faculties. We will look back to another instance that yields the same result, on analysis. When Aeneas first approaches the waters of Acheron, Charon bids him retire, and exclaims,

> 'Umbrarum hic locus est, somni noctisque soporae:
> Corpora viva nefas Stygia vectare carina.'[2]

Once more we have the greater effect of the spoken word—the vividness added from the qualities of both minds, the speaker and the listener. Virgil strikes a modern note because the interest of his inner being predominates over his material; and this is confirmed by the few facts known of his life. It is thought he was of Celtic race, and he loved nature and solitude. He did visit Rome, and became the friend of the Emperor Augustus and of Maecenas, but he rather shrank from the court and social life. His last wish, that the unfinished *Aeneid* should be destroyed, shows his passion for perfection.

Virgil's secret, therefore, is more likely to be found in his 'infinite pity' than his 'canonization of Rome as a sort of living being'[3]: the ultimate impression from Homer is joy: his heroes love life and are at ease on earth; but from Virgil it is sorrow. Happiness does not seem to enter into the Virgilian plan, and even his dwellers in Elysium are not

[1] *Ibid.* 670–1: 'For his sake have we come here, and crossed the great rivers of Erebus.'

[2] *Ibid.* 390–1: 'This is the place of shades, of sleep, and night that brings sleep. It is forbidden to convey living bodies in the Stygian boat.'

[3] Mackail.

exactly happy, despite the beauty of their scene—or, at most, theirs is a negative happiness that comes from duty to the State well done and absence of self-reproach. We can believe that Aeneas loved Creusa, 'in the old days of peace before the Greeks came to Troy',[1] because his was one of those 'grave natures, led by custom, and therefore constant, and likely to be a loving husband', of whom Bacon writes; but we can hardly believe that his heart was set on fire by Dido. He was too preoccupied with his divine mission and oppressed by the difficulties in his path. This oppression of the soul by the weight of earthly things, to the exclusion of joy in life, is at the centre of Virgil's work. The shadow on his mind of a later historical age, the echoes that never entirely fade away of men's evil dealings with each other, withhold him from that silent upper sphere of poetry where Homer dwells. Homer's genius is mighty enough to gather the world in its sweep and rise above it. Virgil selects and excludes before he can transmute; his personal sensibility confines him. He knows how the world can hurt; there is a reserve of individual preference even in his universal pity for mankind. The cry of anguish of Palinurus[2]—that he feared less for himself than his master's ship deprived of its steersman in the rising seas—is a direct pulse of Virgil's heart.

Can the soul extricate itself for a moment from the cares of earth, and shine with its own light? If so, there is to be found Virgil's faith. He had, as we have seen, the mystic power which he imparts to the soul of transforming outer things, of making far-extended tracts of land and ocean greater and more perilous. Surely this inward, 'modern' power should reach its climax in the effect of souls upon each other. The one argument used by Aeneas for abandoning Dido that rings true is the nightly visitation of his father's spirit.[3] The failure (if one dare use such a word in writing about Virgil) to make Aeneas credible as the lover of Dido excludes one resource. There remain the two supreme scenes of the appari-

[1] *Iliad*, XXII. 156. [2] VI. 351–4. [3] IV. 351–3.

tion of Creusa and the reunion with Anchises, and to these we must add the world-sorrow of the speech of Palinurus to Aeneas in the lower regions, rising to personal lament at his enforced detention this side the Styx, and beseeching his help: almost consoled by the thought of funeral honours and the headland that shall keep his name alive in the hearts of men.[1] Although this promise of 'the mound and pillar' is one of Virgil's many borrowings from Homer (*Iliad*, XVI. 457), he has made it imaginatively his own, and touched it with a more homely pathos. In passages of this kind we see how, unlike the early Greek thinkers with their exclusive pride of culture, he voices the democratic message of human brotherhood which was first given to the world by the Stoic philosophy, and prepared the way for Christianity, and we understand why he was accepted by the medieval Church as 'a soul that is naturally Christian', when all other pagan literature was forbidden fruit.

In this recognition of one soul by another, the sharer of past sorrows rather than past joys, yet the one thing that has made it possible to progress so far along life's hard road, we find Virgil's message. It is momentary consolation rather than assurance of any future happiness, and is no sooner found than lost again in the turmoil. Yet in these cross signals there is something immortal, some conviction that the soul's true home is with God. That two persons should have loved each other is an ultimate and self-sufficient fact, above the storm of seas and rage of men. When the Sibyl asks Musaeus about the dwelling of Anchises, and he replies, 'Nulli certa domus',[2] the words produce a mystic silence that Dante has not equalled when he puts the same words into the mouth of Sordello.[3] It is a faith that renews itself in sleep or dreams rather than waking life; it will not inspire its holder to great earthly deeds, since duty to the State is

[1] VI. 337–83.
[2] VI. 673: 'No one has a fixed home'.
[3] *Purgatorio*, VII. 40: 'Loco certo non c'è posto'.

self-compelling and looks for no reward; but it is more than 'an anxious wish, a great perhaps'. Also we remember how the weapons and horses and chariots of the Trojan heroes in the Elysian fields are beautiful in proportion to the care which their owners bestowed on them on earth.[1] If earthly things, then, are symbols of Elysian things, it may also be that earthly meetings and reunions have their counterpart in worlds beyond. It may be true, as Myers said, that 'the anguish of all partings' is conveyed to us through the music of Virgil's lines, but so is the remembrance of all reunions. I say 'remembrance' rather than 'joy', for those who meet are soon to part again. It is thus when his former comrades in arms recognize Aeneas in the shades. To see him is not enough: they must walk beside him and learn the causes of his coming.[2] Though the struggle of life is hard, and the nature of earth and matter intractable, and the wastes of sea far-spread, there is something in the love of human beings for each other that bids us hope. Often what inspires this love is partnership in danger, need to help one another at a crisis; but the result is that we approach Virgil's kingdom of silence so troubled by memories of man's strife and the tears of things, that the effect is more like a haven of rest than rapture of Paradise. In the end we may compare Virgil with the astronomer who infers the existence of a new planet but cannot make the world share his faith, yet ever and again is encouraged by a dream in the reality of his celestial stranger.

And yet we will not conclude that, except for these soul-greetings, Virgil's world is forsaken of God and given over to the strife of hostile forces, for we detect in him the beginning of that feeling for nature which rose to a height in after ages with such writers as Bunyan, Charlotte Brontë, Thomas Hardy. The world of Homer was blessed by God even in its battles of men and deserts of sea. This is not to deny mystery to the long sea journey of Odysseus to the limits of the world, the great stream Oceanus, the land of Cimmerian darkness

[1] *Aeneid*, VI. 653–5. [2] VI. 487–8.

—but it is the mystery of beauty. His only hint of 'strangeness' is that passage of overpowering beauty when the sun-god, Helios Hyperion, threatens, if the outrage be not avenged, he will no longer mount the starry heavens and turn again towards earth, but go down to Hades and shine among the dead.[1] Virgil suggests that nature masks the presence or absence of an unseen reality—above all in the sixth book where its absence frustrates the desires of souls. Such are the middle ways overgrown with forest and surrounded by the river Cocytus, the silent far-spread regions of night, the empty dwellings and realms of Dis, the waters of Acheron with their mud banks and boiling gulf, the squalid ferryman and his crazy bark, the souls praying for passage across the river, the nine folds of the river Styx that interpose between the suicides and the upper air to which they would gladly return, the many rivers and vast stretches of forest and marsh that continue to lengthen out behind Aeneas as he advances further into the lowest shades of Erebus—a whole world denied of the sun and steeped in profound night. These regions are dreadful because they are estranged from God: an estrangement which Dante used in the *Inferno* with his greater power.

From the divine sadness and fleeting hope of Virgil, from his visions that throng the ivory gate, we turn to the genial Horace. It may be hard to discover in one who was so well at ease on earth a transcendental strain, but if we accustom our eyes to the world of his masterpiece—the first three books of the *Odes*—there will glimmer, even through its daylight, a shining track. Preoccupation with this world is usually thought to exclude the other, but enjoyment of the present is a form of religion that has been underrated. Horace's name is almost a synonym for good cheer, and in his pages we read of guests with perfumed and garlanded locks reclining at tables, quaffing bowls of stout Falernian, or wine from jars that were sealed and put aside in the consulship of Manlius,

[1] *Odyssey*, XII. 377–83.

contemporaneous with the poet's birth; but he was no advocate of 'Let us eat and drink for tomorrow we die'. The most famous of his counsels was to observe moderation and the golden mean[1]; and even a moralist like Carlyle has observed that evil lies not in the enjoyment of good things but in our moral enslavement by them.

Cardinal Newman, in his letters, writes that the heathen poets were always yearning for some unknown good and higher truth, and could not find it, and Horace in particular tried to solace himself with the pleasures of sense, while a stern inward monitor warned him of the approach of death. Except in the seventh ode of the fourth book—which is outside his best period—where he says that we mortals are but dust and shadow, his melancholy does not strike me as having such depth. The nearest approach to it is the ode on the death of his friend Quintilius,[2] 'whom no prayers to the gods will restore, because on no such terms was he entrusted to this mortal life'; and also—a very different subject—on the young kid whom he will sacrifice, and so destroy the promise of its growing horns that foreshadowed love and strife.[3] Newman's interpretation of Horace must yield to that of Dr. Mackail, who said that he made himself into a man of the world of the best kind and into a gentleman, and he achieved this without high birth or wealth, over-anxiety or ambition, without special intellectual gifts or saintliness of life.[4] There is but one thing here that needs comment, and that is the clause about special intellectual gifts; for it was Frederick Harrison—a worthy critic—who once called Horace the greatest wizard who ever coined language. This faculty was the Archimedes-lever with which Horace moved the world.[5]

[1] *Odes*, II. 10. [2] I. 24. [3] III. 13.

[4] *Classical Studies* (1925), pp. 145–6.

[5] It is interesting to compare Newman's description of a Christian gentleman (*Idea of a University*, Discourse VIII) with Sainte-Beuve's description of the modern form of the old Roman virtue of urbanity (*Causeries*, Vol. III, pp. 53–5).

Even Virgil spoke of the 'irritable race of poets', and the mind of the poet is usually thought to be an arena of contending passions. Horace was the exception: he fashioned life with the same restraint as he fashioned words, and made life and art heighten each other. It is true that he derived social advantage from his connection with Maecenas, but his feelings went far deeper than worldliness, and every ear practised in rhythm can detect the chord of true love and friendship sounding in his lines on Maecenas. Like many poets, he is at his best in personal relations, and his patriotic odes are the least impressive. He had not Virgil's power to make love of country the source of men's love for each other and loving memories of heroes of the past. At his efforts to deify Augustus our minds tend to recall the humour of the Emperor Vespasian on his deathbed, 'I fear I am becoming a god.' It is the same with the odes that recall Rome's past glories and conquests—except that on Regulus (III. 5)—but when he writes of degeneration, and compares the present luxurious youth with his hardy ancestors, we begin to hear his true voice because it touches his philosophy of moderation.

It is, however, in personal relations that he can most instruct us, and we shall see how this perfection extends to the whole world. There is much about love-making in his poems, but he shines as friend not lover. His two most inspired utterances on love have a reminiscent tinge: as when he bids the friend whose betrothed he is praising, suspect not one who has completed his eighth lustrum[1]; or contrasts the tamer mood of one whose hair is whitening, with the hot blood of his prime in Plancus's consulship.[2] He counsels the moderate use of wine, because excess of it may lead to quarrels; and we hear the sound of his deepest chord when he condemns 'sad anger' (*tristes irae*), worse than 'shipwrecking sea' (*mare naufragum*).[3] If he refers to death as 'eternal exile', and adjures his hearers, in lines too familiar

[1] II. 4. [2] III. 14. [3] I. 16.

to quote, not to cherish long hopes, to enjoy today because we are uncertain of tomorrow and even as we converse envious time is fleeting—not to think of the morrow but to count as a gain what this day has brought—yet his was no incurable melancholy. In his best period he was rightly related to life: his soul was therefore expanded to its full, and the man who has found his soul is a stranger to fear and death.

Loyal friendship, the practice of art, and contented enjoyment of moderate possessions, such as the Sabine farm which fell to Horace's share—these things are an excellent school for the soul. He certainly did despise the rabble,[1] but the pride of culture is not altogether a mean one, and such things have been said of Shakespeare. And he shows how evil may be indirectly overcome by contra-development of good. In the solitude of his Sabine farm nature had spoken to him, and his descriptions of nature have the stillness which is poetry's final aim. The mind that is thus informed preserves its quality even through a descending scale of subjects, and he touches with idealism the revels of Roman youth. The beauty of river and waterfall, of mild spring and fruit-bearing autumn, reappears in white arms and shapely necks, in shining hair, and eyes clearer than the evening star. We may conjecture that with Horace style preceded thought, that in sifting his vocabulary, passing words in review, and meditating over finer shades of meaning, the values of the things he was seeking to express became clearer to him. Art thus led him to a fuller understanding of thought and life.

It may sound strange to speak of Horace in the same breath as Christianity, yet when he bids us be satisfied with a little, because peace of mind is not to be bought with jewels or purple or gold,[2] we cannot but think of the command to banish care and take no thought for the morrow. Our Lord regarded anxiety as 'a terrible spiritual disease',[3] and because Horace conquered anxiety the beauty

1 II. 16. 2 *Ibid.*

3 W. R. Matthews, *Christ*, p. 36.

of the world was revealed to him. It is but a step from this to compare him with that most Christian poet Milton, if we wish to follow up the most impressive movement of his mind. Much has been said of Milton's use of proper names that add charm to his verse. Here is one at the very outset of *Paradise Lost*:

> '. . . or, if Sion hill
> Delight thee more, and Siloa's brook that flowed
> Fast by the oracle of God . . .'[1]

We turn his leaves at random, and they spring out upon us:

> '. . . nor that Nyseian isle,
> Girt with the river Triton, where old Cham,
> Whom Gentiles Ammon call and Libyan Jove,
> Hid Amalthea, and her florrid son,
> Young Bacchus, from his stepdame Rhea's eye'.[2]
>
> . . . .
>
> 'From Arachosia, from Candaor east,
> And Margiana, to the Hyrcanian cliffs
> Of Caucasus, and dark Iberian dales'.[3]

The charm begins and ends with himself, for although he paints beautiful pictures, and delights with the music of words, we think more of his own wonderful mind, and the years he has spent on acquiring knowledge. We withdraw with him into his cloistered stillness, or rise for a moment to his Pisgah height and gaze towards a Promised Land that we shall not enter. Now turn to Horace:

> '. . . non opimae
> Sardiniae segetes feraces,
> Non aestuosae grata Calabriae
> Armenta, non aurum aut ebur Indicum . . .'[4]
>
> . . . .

[1] *P. L.*, I. 10–12. [2] *Ibid.* IV. 275–9.
[3] *P. R.*, III. 316–318.
[4] I. 31: 'Not for the rich harvests of fertile Sardinia, not for the pleasant herds of hot Calabria, nor for Indian gold or ivory'.

'Latius regnes avidum domando
Spiritum, quam si Libyam remotis
Gadibus jungas. . . .'[1]

. . . .

'Frustra: nam scopulis surdior Icari . . .'[2]

Here we are less compelled to the poet's mind than propelled from it; less homeward bound than outward bound; we do not wait for riches to be poured into our lap, but go forth to gather them. Seated on his magic carpet we visit in a flash these remote regions; and realize that the world is one. Because his emotion is true and its expression perfect, the whole world comes forward as witness.

Many thinkers have said that doubt can only be relieved by action, but it is less universally impressed upon us that a right use of this world is a means of unconscious apprehension of a world beyond. Horace triumphantly fulfils this condition, and though he has passages of poignant melancholy, he is, when at his best, when his heart expands to its full, exempt from fear. I think his finest ode is the sixth of the second book, and that in the last stanza his voice is most audible down the ages, and it does not falter as he stands, imaginatively, in death's antechamber, a friend at his side. He may utter no conscious hope, but he is without subconscious fear, and he is not lonely:

'Ille te mecum locus et beatae
Postulant arces; ibi tu calentem
Debita sparges lacrima favillam
Vatis amici.'[3]

These are fitting words in which to take leave of Horace, but for a last salute to Virgil we must look forward many

[1] II. 2: 'Thou shalt rule more widely by subduing a greedy heart than by joining Libya to far-off Gades.'

[2] III. 7: 'In vain: for deafer than the cliffs of Icarus . . .'

[3] 'That place and its blessed heights calls both to you and me; there you will sprinkle a deserved tear over the ashes of your poet friend.'

centuries, to his greatest disciple, and a poet even greater than himself:

> 'O anima cortese Mantovana,
> Di cui la fama ancor nel mondo dura,
> E durera quanto il moto lontana'.[1]

[1] Dante, *Inferno*, II. 58–60: 'O courteous Mantuan soul, whose fame still lives in the world, and will live as long as motion lasts'.

III

DANTE

While still holding the belief that all true poetry, both ancient and modern, is inward, we become aware of a change, even a reversal, when we turn to a modern poet; perhaps because, while the goal of poetry is inward, ancient and modern writers approach it from different sides. The ancient poet needed to travel widely in imagination over the earth's surface and create beauty from what he saw; for the modern poet beauty has already been created; it lies darkly revealed in his own soul, haunting him with memories he must struggle to express. The ideal life of the Middle Ages was contemplative, and as we open Dante's *Vita Nuova* we see the page in shadow, we feel the long periods of meditation that have preceded the written word. European poetry arose again in Provence in the twelfth century, after its suppression through the Dark Ages, and the Latin tongue was discarded by the Provençal poets in favour of the vernacular. The works of these poets have hardly survived for their intrinsic merit, but their ideas still interest, notably that of chivalric love which plays so large a part in Dante. Guido Guinicelli, the poet of northern Italy, on whom fell the mantle of the Troubadours, was Dante's immediate predecessor. He sings how love is native to the gentle heart; and the same thought is expressed by Dante in a sonnet of the *Vita Nuova*, and even in the speech of Francesca in the *Inferno*. The less known Giacomino Pugliesi, lamenting his dead mistress, tells how she often called him her sweet friend. The oft-recurring words—kindness, gentleness, courtesy, companionship—reveal the quality of the love of these poets and its absolute separation from the pagan and animal. How nobly Dante thought of 'tenderness' and 'courtesy' we may read in the *Convivio*[1]; and when Beatrice first speaks to Virgil, she alludes to Dante as her 'friend'.[2]

From the welter of the medieval mind there emerged this most beautiful thing—man's chivalric love of woman. It began and ended in thought, for the lover did not wish to marry the beloved, lest the cares of the world should dull her beauty and despiritualize their conversation. Dante and Beatrice never spoke together, but the salutation which she accorded him in the streets of Florence raised him to the heaven of joy, and the denial of it—on report of his unworthy conduct—cut him to the quick. When she first saluted him, he seemed to behold the uttermost boundaries of blessedness, and her salutation became the goal of his desires. All his happiness lay in it, in the sound of her sweet speech and her wonderful smile. It filled his heart with charity, and forgiveness for any person who had ever wronged him: and here we see how close are love and religion. His other ladies charm without detracting from the supremacy of Beatrice. There is the lady midway between his eyes and Beatrice, whom he used as a screen for his secret; there are the sixty beautiful ladies of Florence whose names he introduced in an epistle; the young and gentle lady who died; the lady of most graceful speech; and the lady at the window, fair, young, and wise, whom he feared might please him too much.

The word 'lady' has a charm, as Dante uses it, and he means 'only such as are gentle and not mere women'. It begins with the soul, but spreads to the most outer things, such as the dress of 'subdued and goodly crimson' which Beatrice wore in her ninth year when he first saw her, or the pure white dress in which she appeared again after nine years. Above all in the smile is heaven revealed—as Leonardo,

[1] II. 11. [2] *Inf.* II. 61.

in the sister art of painting, was to show two centuries later; and also in speech, manner, kindness, beauty, and in youth.[1] The poet of the *Odyssey* so loved this earth that its thinning veils, such as the beauty of Calypso and Nausicaa, admitted the light of heaven. In the heart of the medieval poet heaven is already present, and as he moves through the world he recognizes its degrees of revelation in the faces of his fellow pilgrims.

Dante gave poetic form to the whole philosophy, theology, science, and political thought of his age, but our task is to watch for the gleams of his own imagination. The Divine Comedy is the most carefully constructed work of art, with all its parts corresponding and every detail in its place, but in the *Inferno* we are concerned with the shadow cast by the poet himself as he looks down into the abyss. It is plausible to say that hell is a state of mind, and its tortures symbols of remorse, but there is something in us that will not let these desolate regions—this darkness broken by flashes of fire—dissolve in allegory. If the ideal of the Middle Ages was contemplation,[2] this can be infernal as well as celestial, and the medieval mind was visited by terrors that surpassed those of the pagan mind. Virgil makes Aeneas thus begin his story to Dido:

> 'Infandum, Regina, jubes renovare dolorem.'[3]

The effect is rhetorical, and suggests hardships bravely endured on sea and land. Dante takes these words bodily from Virgil and puts them into the mouth of Ugolino, and he adds the whole inner experience of the Dark Ages:

[1] See *Convivio*, III. 8, where Dante likens the eyes and the smile to the balcony where the lady who dwells within the house of the body, namely the soul, shows herself at times, though veiled.

[2] *Ibid.* IV. 17.

[3] *Aeneid*, II. 3: 'You bid me, O Queen, renew unspeakable grief.' Virgil owed this line to Homer (*Odyssey*, VII. 241), but Greek literature was little known in pre-Renaissance Italy, and Dante had not read Homer.

> 'Tu vuoi ch' io rinnovelli
> Disperato dolor che il cor mi preme
> Gia pur pensando, pria ch' io ne favelli.'[1]

The tremor in the voice warns us, like the shocks of an earthquake, that this apparently solid earth may collapse with us into hollows of gloom and fire. We become aware of a gulf of blackness in which the soul has lost itself for a thousand years.

The darkness of the cities by night and the sound of church bells were characteristic of the Middle Ages, and also the haunting fear of death. To many, in their solitude, there was as much fear as hope in the Christian message. Heat, cold, and darkness were three constant terrors: the prayer 'Lighten our darkness' had literal as well as symbolical meaning. Tradition said that Lazarus, after his resurrection, lived the rest of his life in agonized suspense at the thought of a second passage through the dark strait. Meditation, if truly based, can recreate the soul, but otherwise it may lead to madness. In the speech about death which Shakespeare assigns him, Claudio mentions 'lawless and uncertain thought'. Man is inseparable from his environment, and when there is nothing in the outer world to correspond with his thought, the result is chaos. Bunyan desisted from ringing the church bells from fear lest they should fall on his head.

To look into nature and think of the awful things that might exist, and the sins that might be committed, can produce fear beyond anything that the external world can produce. The pagan imagination created terrible shapes, such as the giants whose legs ended in serpents; the Minotaur, part bull, part man; Typhoeus with a hundred serpents' heads; Echidna with the head and bust of a woman, otherwise a serpent; the Chimaera with lion's head, goat's body, and tail ending in a serpent's head. There is a streak of this livid hue in the *Inferno*, and Dante even introduces these fabulous monsters of the ancient world—the Minotaur,

[1] *Inf.* XXXIII. 4–6: 'You wish me to renew desperate grief that wrings my heart even at the thought, before I speak of it.'

Geryon, and the giants Ephialtes and Antaeus who guard the central pit of hell. This kingdom of terrors is no illusion but part of the soul's inheritance. St. Augustine bore witness that in sleep imagination has greater force than reality.

We will consider some of the typical scenes as we descend with Dante and his guide.[1] At the entrance to the first circle he gazes down into a valley so dark, deep, and cloudy that he can see no end, and from it rise infinite wailings. Further on is a place utterly dark, sounding like the sea, tormented with winds that blow to and fro lost souls that shriek and blaspheme. Rain, hail, and snow prevail in the third circle, and spirits howl like dogs. Greater misery awaits as they descend where the Stygian marsh spreads at the foot of the precipice, and the naked, bemired folk are striking and biting each other. The city of Dis rises out of the waters, its mosques glowing with internal fire, surrounded by ditches and iron walls: only the gleam of fire shows in a land of blackness. Heretics fixed in burning tombs with the lids open, from which issue their cries, occupy the sixth circle. The violent are sunk in a river of boiling blood; suicides are confined and rooted in thorn trees; those who defied God or nature lie upon or wander over a horrible plain of sand under a rain of fire. We see figures with sores branded by flame on their limbs; the thunder of a cataract reveals the depth of the abyss down which the next descent must be made; and an awful shape rises on the waters—Geryon, half man, half serpent. Malebolge is a region of ten circles diminishing in circumference as they descend. The valleys are divided by dykes crossed by arched bridges, from the summit of which you look down into depths of darkness only broken by gleams of fire. One of these 'pouches' is full of boiling pitch in which sinners are submerged; and demons who patrol the banks prick with forks those who rise to the surface. The eighth

[1] For detailed exposition of the whole Divine Comedy, see the work in 3 vols. of John S. Carroll: *Exiles of Eternity*, 1903; *Prisoners of Hope*, 1906; *In Patria*, 1911 (Hodder and Stoughton).

pit contains more serpents than Maremma, and Dante sees a man suddenly transformed into a reptile. Here are men with mutilated limbs; and the gashes inflicted by the sword of a demon reunite in order to be renewed. A victim with hands chopped off raises the stumps, and a headless body carries its head in its hand. In the centre of Malebolge opens a pit surrounded by terrific guardian forms, and in its depth is a frozen morass. The shades, fixed in the ice, resemble frogs that croak with their muzzles out of water. The chattering jaws and anguished eyes over which tears have formed a crystal visor, the faces grinning like dogs for the chill, will haunt Dante for ever, so that the sight of a frozen pool in the upper world will at all times cause him a shudder.

It is often said that this idea of hell—fire and darkness and torment—belongs to a vanished superstitious age and does not affect us; but this is not the whole truth. There are regions of the earth that suggest hell—burning, waterless deserts, frozen Arctic spaces, raging seas, inaccessible mountains like Everest, cuirassed with rock and swept by blizzards. There are loathsome beasts and reptiles and insects, and climates where no one can live. There is something in the mind of man that is related to hell, and that makes him a realist and power-politician. The horrors of modern war in Spain and Poland—death rained from above on women and children,[1] populations torn from their homes and deported and put to forced labour, concentration camps, and condemned prisoners made to dig their own graves—all these things prove the truth of Dante's doctrine, that when men live without God there is hell. As he says in the *Convivio* (IV. 7), the sinner is already dead—the man dies and the beast survives.

That man's unhappiness comes of his greatness is an old saying, for he cannot suppress his soul, though he may fail to convert to spirit the part of his soul which communicates

[1] Written in March 1940, before the air attacks on Britain, and long before the revelations of the horrors of the German prison camps.

with God, and his soul warns him that his destiny extends beyond this world. Such terrors as Dante depicts are no primitive legends or old wives' tale, but part of man's mental constitution, and lie in ambush for us if we live without God. The abandoned soul, restricted to earth, is forced to use its immortal powers within earthly limits. Dante's lost souls are not rid of their sins: the violent continue to assault each other; the misers and the lustful are tormented by the same restlessness as in life. Two passages from English writers will help us to understand the spirit of the *Inferno*—Swift's description of the Struldbrugs in *Gulliver's Travels*, and some lines spoken by Beatrice Cenci in Shelley's play. According to Swift, the Struldbrugs were faced with the dreadful prospect of immortality on earth. As years passed on they lost all natural affection, and were afflicted with envy and impotent desires; their envy being chiefly aroused by the vices of the young and the deaths of the old. After eighty they were looked upon as dead in law, and had to surrender their estates to their heirs. They gradually forgot more and more, even the names of their dearest friends. They could not read, because memory failed between the beginning and end of a sentence; and as language changes, after two hundred years they were unable to hold any conversation with their neighbours. They lost their teeth and hair, and all distinction of taste for their food, and were despised and hated by everyone; and the women were more horrible than the men. We know how Swift, in his enforced retirement in Ireland after his short and brilliant political career, consumed his heart with memories. He dreaded solitude, old age, and failing powers, and his nausea was easily awakened by the physical side of life. His soul was mighty but his spirit faint, and as the soul is immortal so are its sufferings. With Beatrice Cenci, the thought that terrifies her when about to die by the executioner is that there may be no God in the void world, and she may meet her father's spirit, the form which had tortured her on earth and was ever present and omnipotent. The *Inferno*, then, is no relic of a bigoted age, but something that touches the modern mind most nearly. When man denies God he finds something in nature that drives him mad with fear, and his imagination shapes forms of monstrous horror.

It is the modern fashion not only to reject hell but also responsibility for sin. Crime is thought a disease, or the effect of bad surroundings, and the criminal one who should be nursed back to mental health. We tolerate our sins, and ascribe them to temperament or heredity, beyond our control; or we boast of them as the consequences of fullness of life and self-development. It is censured as morbid to brood over sin and lament a past beyond recall, and more likely to enfeeble than strengthen the character. Dante, however, makes will supreme, and as we approach the Mount of Purgatory, after passing through the circles of the Inferno, we realize the break between those who are excluded from God and those who have turned to God, even if they have deferred it till the moment of death.[1]

The souls destined for Purgatory assemble on the sacred island at the mouth of the Tiber, and are conveyed across the sea by the Angel Pilot. They approach the lower slopes of the mountain, and struggle upward to the first of the seven terraces that surround it, on each of which a sin is expiated. When Dante has surmounted the terraces, Virgil, who typifies human reason, leaves him. At the summit is the Earthly Paradise, and there takes place the procession of the Church, after which Beatrice, who typifies Revelation, appears to prepare him for the ascent to heaven. The element of autobiography, with which we are concerned,

[1] 'Any candid person can verify the significance and power of sin by invoking the threefold testimony of man's moral judgment, as revealed in his literature, his history, and his conscience. . . . A sense of sin is not only expressed in all great literature worthy the name; it is a creative element therein' (J. S. Whale, 'Sin and the Need of Redemption' in *The Christian Faith*, ed. W. R. Matthews, p. 193).

most prevails in the *Purgatorio*, where heaven and earth are nearer related; and because of this interaction the reader will find purer poetry here than in the gloom of the *Inferno* or the light of the *Paradiso*.

The climax of the *Purgatorio* is the draught of Lethe which takes away remembrance of sin; for sin must not only be expiated but forgotten. This is a hard thought, and we recall a sentence from Donne's sermon on the Day of Judgment: 'There thou shalt see, to thine inexpressible terror, some others cast down into hell for thy sins which they would not have done but upon thy provocation'. Yet we also recall the words of David in Psalm li, after his betrayal of Uriah: 'Against Thee only have I sinned'; and we must be content to leave the problem of our duty to God and man unsolved. There are recorded instances of men who have committed the deadliest sins and, by true repentance, re-attained peace and happiness. No poet exceeds Dante in tenderness, and he was ever perplexed by the problem of the virtuous heathen, excluded from heaven through no fault of their own; nor was he himself a stranger to 'the sting of remembrance'.[1] If, then, we accept his guidance, we must believe with him that when the soul, by purification, has become spirit, it returns to God, and sin is as alien to its nature as it is to God.[2]

The opening scene of the *Paradiso* is set in the Earthly Paradise, on the summit of the Mount of Purgatory. All things desire union with God, and now that the will is purified, movement towards God is natural, and Dante is not aware that he is rising. With Beatrice he enters the heaven of the Moon that surrounds them like a pearl, and they glide into it as a ray of light penetrates smooth water. There dwells

[1] *Purg.* XII. 20.

[2] 'The fully forgiven man does not rejoice in his own forgiven-ness but in the divine love to which he owes it; and his past sin persists in his experience no longer as a source of shame but as the occasion of a new wonder in his adoration of the love divine' (William Temple, *Nature, Man and God*, p. 423).

Piccarda Donati, who is content with her station in the lowest heaven because such is the will of God. The next stage is Mercury, which grows brighter as Beatrice enters. At each ascent her smile becomes more beautiful, and by this sign Dante knows he is progressing. The Emperor Justinian now discourses on Roman law, and vindicates Dante's theory of the divine mission of the Roman Empire. In Venus, Charles Martel discourses on degeneration and the folly of opposing nature, in forcing religion on one who would fight, or kingship on the would-be preacher. Cunizza and Folco of Marseilles utter their prophecies; and the spirit of Rahab appears like a ray of the sun trembling in water—admitted to that sphere because she helped Joshua in the holy cause. The shadow of earth touches these lowest heavens. The spirits that inhabit there truly served God, but made their service a means also of winning earthly renown.

In the heaven of the Sun, Dante speaks with Aquinas, his master in theology, who shows him the spirits of Albertus Magnus, Gratian, Orosius, Boethius, and many others. The Cross of Mars flashes a redder glow, and from arm to arm and base to summit the lights of spirits are moving. Cacciaguida, Dante's ancestor, recalls to him the ancient simplicity and modern degeneration of Florence, and prophesies to him his exile with its inevitable sorrows. The increasing transfiguration of Beatrice, in the mystic Eagle of Jupiter, almost overwhelms Dante, and she needs to remind him that Paradise is not in her eyes alone. Divine justice becomes the subject of discourse, and Dante's preoccupying care for the virtuous heathen who knew not Christ. The beauty of the Cross in Mars, of the Eagle in Jupiter, is eclipsed by the Golden Ladder in Saturn, down whose rungs move splendours that outshine the stars. In conversation with St. Peter Damian, Dante seeks in vain to probe the most insoluble of all mysteries—what is the cause of our meeting with some few selected persons out of the great multitude of creation? A sign from Beatrice, and they have topped the ladder and are in the Heaven of the Stars. Once more she bids him take less thought for her and gaze upon his divine surroundings. St. Peter examines him on faith, St. James on hope, St. John on love. In the Crystalline Heaven with its circles of light, Beatrice expounds the nature of the Celestial Intelligences. There follow the heavens of pure light, intellectual light full of love, a river of light. Dante drinks of this river, and then sees the two Courts of Heaven and the splendour of God. Beatrice returns to her place among the blessed, and in the care of St. Bernard he prepares for the ultimate vision. He sees the Apostles and Saints and Fathers, and hears the prayer to the Virgin Mother. Last of all are the three circles that symbolize by their eternal motion the peace of those whose wills are one with God.

Such is a brief outline of Dante's progress, omitting the historical, theological, and cosmological speculations by the way. Not that the vast body of learning has failed to become music at his touch—as often in the work of Lucretius—but we are here concerned with the autobiographical thread. In the *Inferno* we saw the soul excluded from God; in the *Purgatorio* the soul returning to God and enduring its punishment gladly; and in the *Paradiso* we see the soul ever growing in knowledge and love of God. Many readers have been deterred from the *Faerie Queene* by the imperfectly managed allegory, in spite of Hazlitt's comment that 'the allegory will not bite them'; but this need not apply to Dante. No doubt, as with all the greatest writers, the more knowledge the more appreciation, and there is much in the *Paradiso* that still puzzles Dante's own countrymen; yet the ordinary wayfaring Christian, unversed in the refinements of scholastic thought, will not approach Dante in vain.

It has pleased some commentators to make Beatrice a symbol of theology, and decide that she reproached Dante not for moral lapses but devotion to secular instead of sacred learning. We prefer to think of her as a human being, and of the *Paradiso* as the last expression of the thought outlined in the *Vita Nuova*. Like all great men and poets Dante was simple at heart, and although the poet of Catholicism, he was often unorthodox. He cared for the heathen, he condemned the Papal decrees, and he favoured the views of the Calabrian Abbot Joachim,[1] who anticipated an era of the Spirit when the Church with its rites and sacraments should be no more. From Christianity downwards the greatest devotion and sacrifices have been called forth by the person, not the cause. The representative human being, therefore, not doctrine, is the core of his inspiration. He proves to us by the super-logic of poetry, by the ever more unveiled beauty of Beatrice, that what we love in our fellow creatures is God. This high knowledge does not alienate him from the world, as it did Milton, but increases his love for it. From a touch like this,

> 'Come l'augello intra l' amate fronde,
> Posato al nido dei suoi dolci nati',[2]

to the height where he sees God rejoicing in the face of Beatrice,[3] he reveals how love is the prime mover of the universe. We may think of the mighty 'thunder-roll' of Homer's verse, of its incomparable 'slide'; or of Shakespeare's 'fine-filed phrase'; but we never separate Dante from his complete message.

The fate of a book in the minds of its readers often differs from the author's intention. Sir Charles Sherrington says that 'the mind's earthliness innately shapes all it does, perhaps most so when it tries to be unearthly'. He quotes Socrates, who delighted in conversation, and who 'to imagine paradise . . . thus invokes its favourite pursuit from earth and a custom of earth's social creature, man'.[4] It pleased Socrates to think that if death was something more than a

[1] *Par.* XII. 40.
[2] *Par.* XXIII. 1–2: 'As a bird among the beloved leaves, at peace in the nest with its sweet offspring'.
[3] *Par.* XXVII. 105.
[4] *Man on his Nature* (1940), pp. 165–6.

dreamless sleep, if it was a change and migration of the soul from this to another place, he would have the chance of meeting with Orpheus and Musaeus and Hesiod and Homer, and with the great heroes and statesmen and leaders of armies of the past. In conversing and associating with them and examining them, he would find immeasurable happiness. And so, in spite of Dante's supernatural imaginings, he reveals the most precious things about himself when he touches earth. None of his descriptions of places in hell or purgatory or heaven come home so nearly as those that recall us to the world we know—to the mountains and rivers and cities and roads of Italy, to the coasts and islands of the Mediterranean. In the *Inferno* the sepulchres of the heretics are like those at Arles near the Rhone (IX. 112 ff.); the suicides' wood is compared with Maremma—that region of swamp and forest and snakes and stagnant water (XIII. 7 ff.); one of the gulfs of Malebolge recalls the Arsenal at Venice with its boiling and tenacious pitch (XXI. 7 ff.); all the pain and diseases of the hospitals of Valdichiana, Maremma, and Sardinia are concentrated in the last gulf of Malebolge (XXIX. 46–51). Nothing in the stories of the damned is more sinister than the details they give of their final passage: how devils took charge of their souls at the moment of death and consigned them to this or that circle of hell. It is a terrible thought that after his soul's departure to the lowest circle the body of Branca d'Oria remained on earth inhabited by a demon (XXXIII. 140 ff.).

In the first canto of the *Purgatorio* Dante reminds Cato of his earthly love Marzia, and it is sad to hear that Marzia can no longer affect him. Manfred (III. 103–45) begs Dante to recall him to his daughter Costanza and ask her prayers, since much can be done by those on earth for souls in purgatory. Buonconte fears that his wife Giovanna has forgotten him (V. 89); and Nino Visconti asks that his daughter Giovanna may pray for him, since her mother has forgotten him (VIII. 70–5). 'If you ever tread again the Tuscan soil', says Sapia, 'recall me to those who were nearest to me' (XIII. 149–50). Forese Donati confesses that he owes his advancement to the prayers and sighs of his Nella, who is dear and pleasing to God (XXIII. 85 ff.). At the sweet sound of his native city, Sordello runs to embrace Virgil (VI. 73–80). In the second canto Dante renews with Casella memories of the song of love (*amoroso canto*), the sweetness of which still haunts him; and in the twenty-sixth he recognizes Guido Guinicelli, his forerunner and instructor in the gracious art of poetry. Dante himself never forgets his noble descent or the 'fine style' (*bello stile*) which has brought him much honour.[1] Even in the *Paradiso* the inhabitants of the heaven of Mars (XIV), who appear like flames, remember their bodies and think of their parents and dear ones. Francesca, and Beatrice also, speak of the beautiful forms that were theirs on earth.[2]

So far we have dealt with the horror which this world adds to hell, or the homesickness it inspires in purgatory, but now we will witness to its share in the final joy. Dante's leading characteristic was sensitiveness to his fellow creatures, as we saw in the *Vita Nuova* when he was shaken to the depths by the salutation of Beatrice; and on one occasion the effect on him of her presence was such that the company broke out in laughter, and a certain person afterwards said to him, 'Unto what end lovest thou this lady, since her very presence overwhelms thee?' We will recall that, in the fashion of the Troubadours, marriage was not the goal of this love, lest earth's familiarities should corrupt. On the other side, the greatest sorrow of his exile was the 'evil and stupid' race of men with whom he was compelled to associate.[3] We will therefore conclude that the highest beauty of his poem is in the meetings of the world's finest souls—in such passages as these: 'I am Beatrice'; 'I am Lucia'; 'I am Sordello'; 'I was called

[1] *Par.* XVI. 1–6; *Inf.* I. 87.
[2] *Inf.* V. 101; *Purg.* XXXI. 30–1.
[3] *Par.* XVII. 61–3.

Cunizza'; 'Because I am more beautiful you will not fail to recognize me as Piccarda'[1]; 'I lived in Rome in the time of the good Augustus'; 'Are you Virgil, fountain of that great river of speech? Honour and light of all poets . . .'[2]; 'The people still call me Statius. I sang of Thebes, and of the great Achilles'.[3] This beauty is intellectual, the beauty of knowledge, something that has been withheld from the simple and revealed to the wise. In the recognitions and responses of these beings, in their self-revealings and courteous speech, there is a note of wonder, of interrogation. They are strangers, or long parted, or known to each other by fame or hearsay, but love arises spontaneously, or old loves are renewed without an effort. If the heaven of Socrates was conversation, that of Dante was communion, for Socrates was still concerned with life as it is. Socrates wished to discover who among the inhabitants of the next world was wise, and who thinks he is when he is not, and he conjectured that he will not be condemned for such activities there as he has been here. At the approach of Dante's glorified beings, at the beam which they cast before them, we are overthrown, as he was by the salutation of Beatrice, or Shelley by the vision of intellectual beauty. Life's greatest experience is perception of the divine in a fellow creature—the flash of revelation that we and they are children of God, created for love. But here too there is quality, and Dante's characters are the elect of the elect because they have converted soul to spirit by means of earth's finest products—art, philosophy, genius, even personal beauty—and though they partake of heavenly blessings, they do not forget earth, their common mother. They make lights in memory like the figures in the east windows of shadowed cathedrals, whose eyes see far-off things and whose heads are aureoled.

[1] *Par.* III. 48–9. [2] *Inf.* I. 71 ff. [3] *Purg.* XXI. 91–2.

IV

SHAKESPEARE

If Shakespeare is for all time he is also of an age, and his age was the Renaissance, and in combining his Renaissance traits we may best arrive at a personal view. Preoccupation with the life beyond had yielded to interest in this life and discovery of its beauty; and though there was a revival of paganism, the Christian interval left its mark. The heavenly beauty which the Italian painters bestowed upon sacred figures was transferred to those of the world about them, the body became the symbol and interpreter of the soul. In Italy the spirit of self-conscious freedom, the courage of men to be themselves either for good or evil, produced a race of glorious human beings. The final product of art and scholarship was a courtesy of speech and manner which spread through Europe, and in England was realized in Shakespeare and the drama.

Shakespeare was a romantic; in his comedies the inner spirit predominated over the outer situation. Their message is delight in society, love, friendship, the opportunities for kindness in human intercourse, the confidence of men and women in each other. The two groups of *Love's Labour's Lost* are ready at once to be friends and lovers; there is nothing unkind in the interchange of wit, but joy from the exercise of their faculties. The King's death unites the lovers by suspending mock hostility and by revealing them truly bound to each other. The emotion is shared by all the members of the groups, who have no secrets from each other in a world given over to love and marriage. It is especially gracious because the various couples are friends as well as lovers. To deny that this young and golden world represents Shakespeare's state of mind is to push scepticism to its furthest limits.

Shakespeare's romanticism is even more salient in *Verona* because it weakens his dramatic power. In *Love's Labour's Lost* the wit of Berowne was a safeguard, but in *Verona* the surrender by Valentine of Silvia to Proteus has long offended critics. What may be a technical mistake is compensated by the knowledge it affords of Shakespeare's self—the rush of emotion that obliterated all else when soul comes within sight of soul, the belief that not only lovers but friends have all things in common. The touch of reality comes from the heart-utterances of Julia that express how blank to the young is a world without love. It is the same of Adriana's reproachful speeches in the *Errors*, with all its fantastic situations, good humour, and delight of human beings in mutual entertainment. Adriana voices regret for betrayed friendship and kindness ill-requited, and apprehension for the havoc time can play with youth and love. *Midsummer Night's Dream* is the most perfect as drama so far, because the constitution of the fairy world was closer akin to Shakespeare at this time than the real world, and the balance between inner and outer is more perfect; although the marvellous prevails and fairies work their will on 'human mortals', yet a human truth lies at the core. Love is the necessity of happiness, but the magic herb is a symbol of the state of mind of one for whom happiness is a natural inheritance but who is seduced by desire for change: one who has grown to youth amid fair surroundings, courted a maiden, and then, because life is all joy, tires of his joy. He looks upon his friend's mistress and sees that she is fair, and the result is brief madness and recrimination, followed by repentance. It is summer lightning in the clear sky of that English countryside whose surpassing loveliness was the foundation of Shakespeare's life.

The evil in the *Merchant of Venice* is still something remote from life, despite the power with which Shylock is portrayed and the justice of his resentment against Antonio. It suggests the dragon or evil fairy used to frighten children, to make them more conscious of their security, which when out of sight is also out of memory. The poetic heart of the play is love and romantic friendship, and these things are so vivid that they overcome the requirements of the material world. According to the Marxian standards of some modern critics, Bassanio was a parasite and waster, and therefore unworthy of Portia; but we surrender to his courteous manner and delight in his success. Antonio is reputed a thriving merchant, but, royally careless of his money, at any moment he would sacrifice the needs of business to those of friendship. That these characters ring true proves that the finer world in which Shakespeare moved is no illusion. He even makes us believe in the legality of the bond for a pound of flesh and the duty of the State to enforce it.

The three plays *Much Ado*, *Twelfth Night*, *As You Like It* are the zenith of Shakespeare's comedy—the wit of Beatrice, the delicacy of Viola, the love-prate of Rosalind. If we compare *Much Ado* with *Love's Labour's Lost*, we notice a light shadow on the page—a hint of that evil which is not external but secreted by human nature. It is the rumour that Don Pedro, professing to woo Hero for Claudio, has wooed for himself; but the cloud is soon dispelled. The minds of the persons are less open to the world than in the youthful play, less confident that all mankind are ready to participate in their joy. The wit is more salted, and the reader is not untouched by fear that it may pass into unkindness: yet love is the grand disposer of events. It needs but a slender plot to make Benedick and Beatrice drop their mock hostility and embrace as lovers; though we do feel the drag of the outer world when the unworthy Claudio, in the words of Dr. Johnson, is dismissed to happiness. *Twelfth Night* is a feast of love, where the individual is subordinate. Sebastian is easily exchanged for the disguised Viola, and Viola for Olivia; Viola, who loves the Duke, pleads his cause with

Olivia; Antonio will risk his life rather than part with his new-made friend Sebastian. So long as there is beauty and kindness, no need for personal traits formed in the stress of life. The romantic incidents of the shipwreck, Viola's disguise, Antonio's sea fight, mingle with the dreams of the lovers, half real, half imaginary, as luxurious-living persons, who touch the earth but lightly, are apt to confuse the facts of daily existence with their readings in romance. The disappointment of Malvolio is a contrast, but in minds brimful of happiness there is no room for the sorrows of the defeated. Rosalind and Orlando, Celia and Oliver, in *As You Like It*, love at first sight. At the touch of the forest Duke Frederick and Oliver are converted, their past misdeeds forgotten. Rosalind's love is all tenderness, and when, disguised as a youth, she bids Orlando call her 'Rosalind', we can imagine her meditating fondly on the self-conscious accent the name will have on the lips of her lover who thinks she is not Rosalind.

The central emotion of all these plays is the delight of human beings in each other, but their spirit is not pagan. The inheritance of the Middle Ages could not be dismissed in a generation, and though other-worldliness has no place, the habit of reverie is transferred from things heavenly to things earthly. To fix the thoughts exclusively on the supernatural is to lose interest in the natural, and here just so much interest is sacrificed as to subserve the highest art and irradiate with heavenly beauty the places where men and women congregate. When persons dare to be themselves either for good or evil, they incline to play fast and loose with material things, to the scandal of the orderly citizen. This strain appears in the early romantic Shakespeare, and will appear also in the middle regions of his work—*e.g.* Falstaff—and it makes us acquiesce in the fortune-hunting of Bassanio, the sudden friendship of Antonio and Sebastian (*T.N.*), the readiness of Antonio (*M.V.*) to sacrifice business interests and everything else for the sake of friendship; it makes us close our eyes to the reality of evil and forget disappointments. We only stumble at the self-sacrifice of Valentine and the restoration of Claudio. We note also the omnipresence of love, and the ease with which it is transferred from one individual to another, because it is the atmosphere of this young world and comes unsought rather than hardly won. These Renaissance figures excel because they respond to the beauty of God's creation in each other—features, voice, manner, address, the comfort of human companionship. They are rid of other-worldly terrors, but they have not so long left their Father's house as to be forgetful of His teaching of the unimportance of material things, especially when love is weighed against earthly treasure or men's opinion.

The evil in *Romeo and Juliet* that proves fatal to the lovers is still something accidental rather than part of man's constitution. Montagu seems a good man, and neither Capulet nor even Tybalt are really bad; the feud between the two houses has external causes, and the crimes committed are those of sudden impulse and passion. Yet the reality of love, the emptiness of all other earthly things compared with love, is better conveyed because the lovers are members of hostile families. Shakespeare has progressed no further with this theme, and we believe Romeo's words to the Friar:

> 'Do thou but close our hands with holy words,
> Then love-devouring death do what he dare;
> It is enough I may but call her mine.'

The dome of many-coloured glass becomes more beautiful than the white radiance of eternity.

We find little of Shakespeare in the three *Henry VI* plays, except the passion in the second and third parts which vitalizes Gloucester, Margaret, and the King himself—and in the scene where Say pleads for his life with Cade. *Richard III* is Marlowesque: the prevailing note is the pride of earthly life. The true Shakespearian quality is absent because the characters are not connected emotionally. We believe that Richard enacted wonders at Bosworth, but his ghostly visitants on the eve of battle convey no feeling of awe. *King John* is the first historical play to be stamped with the master's seal, and in one passage it is unsurpassed. All through we feel the underworking of the human mind against the actions in the outer world which it has set in motion. Power and material possessions are the prizes, and although conscience revolts, these things have gained such momentum that conscience fails, like a swimmer drawn irresistibly by the outgoing tides to his doom. The play's great scene is where Hubert describes to the King the terror that sweeps the land at the report of Arthur's death (IV. 6), because it fulfils the ideal of history and shows how king, nobles, gentry, people are a social structure where each has a part in ensuring the general safety. When crime is suspected in the royal house there is fear that the whole will submerge; whereas the glories of the *Henry IV*'s are the portraits of individuals. The politics of *Richard II* are of the negative kind, and Richard fails because he is insensitive to the needs of practical life. He mistakes his own wishes for the laws of nature, and brushes aside the arguments of York against despoiling Bolingbroke. When ruin comes, he draws on his reserves of self-pity, and takes pleasure in expressing his sorrow in fine words and adorning it with metaphors from life and history. It fortifies him like a stimulant, and enables him to meet his enemies face to face, but the contrast is too glaring between his lyrical strains and the strength of organized rebellion.

With the two plays of *Henry IV* we regain the true Renaissance Shakespeare and his delight in the banquet of life. As history they never touch the point in *John* where for a moment he realized the mystical unity of the nation and revealed its soul. Here it is the individual that outstands, and the story of his mind interests more than the events. Glendower and Hotspur are poets as well as men of action; the first, with his supernatural intuitions, was afterwards to be more fully shown as Macbeth; the second, with his power to idealize the pageant of war, as Othello. Both are more at ease in the upper regions of the imagination than the world of earthly reality. Glendower, as we know from the effect on Hotspur, was an excessive talker, and so was Hotspur, though he condemned the habit in others. In this age a thing is not fulfilled unless others know it. To do one's duty before God hardly suffices without the approval of God's very able representative, Man. There must be a round table and seats for the actors in life's drama where they are made immortal by speech. With Hotspur war is the nurse of friendship, and had he survived, he would have doffed his armour and spent life's evening with former comrades in arms, and honourable foes, now friends, in discoursing of past battles.

In life we would shrink from a person who robbed travellers and told falsehoods, but Falstaff does these things and delights us. He does not expect his excuses about Gadshill to be believed, as Bradley said; but such is the power of his humour, the depth of his enjoyment of pleasures of sense, and expectation of more when his friend the Prince shall be king, that he hints at a transcendental region where mind exists but material things no longer count—and so spellbinds the reader. To call his state religious may sound a mockery, yet the grape is God's gift to man, and if its use so stimulates the intellectual faculties as to make the meetings in the tavern seem like heaven, we can forget the moral consequences, because time does not exist for immortal spirits. The world is young, man is still part-conscious of his divine origin, newly conscious of the joy of exploring the minds of his equally divine fellow creatures. It is not rash to say that this belief in friendship was Shakespeare's own, that here it overweighted historic and dramatic truth, for the rejection of Falstaff finds the reader unprepared, despite the explanations of critics—except Bradley, who said truly that the result is unsatisfactory and it was not Shakespeare's intention to inflict so great a shock.

There are passages in II *Henry IV* that depress the reader

from the imaginative heights and restore the values of the dark world, such as Prince John's treachery to the rebels, Falstaff's appropriation of a thousand pounds from Shallow, and—most of all—the rejection of Falstaff; because the facts of history were uncongenial to Shakespeare, and in seeming to justify breach of friendship he was committing high treason against himself. *Henry V*, where the cause prevails and the persons are secondary, lacks the finest Shakespearian quality. In this atmosphere of patriotism and statesmanship, only the man of action can breathe, who is implacable to the enemy, scornful of the shirker. He is brother to him who does his duty, no matter what his social position, but he has no time for romantic feelings, and leaves old friends who are not efficient, like Falstaff, to die in obscurity. Hotspur and his fellows did wrong, but they came trailing clouds of glory that eclipse the sober livery of the orthodox patriots of this play.

The two plays that precede the tragedies—*All's Well* and *Measure for Measure*—mark the appearance of evil, especially the first, though it abounds in patchwork and verse of different periods. In Bertram's pride of birth which, for him, outweighs true goodness and betrays him into slander and perjury, we see the beginning of alienation from God and effects of man's inhumanity to man. Yet the magic of Shakespeare touches the play with final peace and beauty, by means of the kindness rising like a well-spring in the heart of Helena, extending to the Countess, Lafeu, the King, the widow and her daughter, perhaps in the end to Bertram. The plot of *Measure for Measure* is improbable, the psychology of Angelo questionable, the reconciliations extravagant, yet it is only just below Shakespeare's greatest because of the philosophic speeches and gnomic sayings of the characters. The destiny of man, Shakespeare implies, is greater than he knows, and while he spends his time in petty traffickings and idle speech, awful forces are at work around. Now and then he suspects their presence and, with a shudder, hides his head in the sand; or, like a child, begs for a little more time to play; or, like the Sluggard, for yet a little more sleep, a little more slumber, a little more folding of the hands in sleep. Claudio was set on pleasure when death stared him in the eyes. There is an old story that, in the days before scientific navigation, when ships sailed close to shore, a ship's crew and company were suddenly warned by clouds of foam and wheeling albatrosses that they were being drawn into the ocean, and they cried out in terror to the steersman to port the helm and return to the familiar gulf. . . . Claudio's great speech is agnostic, but the play as a whole leaves the impression that death is the end of all. The one reconciling influence in a sick world is the Duke, who is quintessentially Shakespearian.

The characters of *Julius Caesar* live politically rather than in their inner selves, though as we near the end we realize the true friendship of Brutus and Cassius. It was not always proof against the shocks of the outer world; it sometimes lacked correspondence between inner emotion and outer fact, and was based on the admiration of the impulsive Cassius for a greater spirit; but it turns to pure gold at the moment of parting. The verse is more rhetorical than mystical; these two lines of Horatio's surely convey to us the majesty of Rome more than the whole of *Julius Caesar*:

> 'In the most high and palmy state of Rome,
> A little ere the mightiest Julius fell . . .'

and so we pass on to *Hamlet*.

Hamlet is the bridge between the two halves of Shakespeare's work—the world where evil was something of a stranger, and that wherein it plays a full part. Hamlet, a child of the Renaissance, rejoicing in the glory of life and touching it at all points—courtier, scholar, soldier, friend, lover—sees the collapse of the whole social framework of his life. His love for his father bordered upon worship; we feel his temporary relief from heaviness when he opens his heart to Horatio; in the kindness of his greeting to Rosencrantz and Guildenstern there is a faint revival of the past, of something saved from the wreck. His voice has homesickness in it when he describes his father's noble presence or recalls his memories of Yorick. Moralists condemn grief as a selfish passion because it unfits people for the duties of life. All grief, Max Müller said, is sweet remembrance of past happiness; and the Dante–Boethius quotation is familiar to everyone. According to Trollope, he was a wise man who prayed, 'Let me ever remember my living friends, but forget them as soon as dead.'[1] Hamlet in health and strength was the finest flower of the Renaissance—restored pagan freedom and beauty, with added grace of God—but he needed a rich earthly soil, and when the drought came he withered. His quick changes from softness to violence are an infallible Renaissance trait, and may be paralleled by the reverse order in Macbeth, who, in the moment of murdering Duncan, would answer 'Amen' to the groom's prayer for a blessing. He was overthrown by the revelation of human wickedness —first his mother's conduct, and secondly the murder of his father. Thus we see the beginning of the struggle between good and evil; also a kind of anxious foreboding that, as the centuries progress, God may withdraw further and abandon the world to the forces of evil.

The terror of Othello's passion must not make us forget his love of life and imaginative anticipation of the Promised Land of happiness. His ancestors were men of royal siege, he thought himself no whit inferior to the Venetian senators, but a life of warfare had denied him their softer accomplishments. In his heart he carried the germ of this finer knowledge; in moments of leisure he watched with a poet's eye the processes of nature. The courtesy of his address shows a being unsubdued to the rough material in which it had

[1] I do not myself like Trollope's sentiment. I prefer that of William Penn about lost friends: 'If absence be not death, neither is theirs; death is but crossing the world, as friends do the seas; they live in one another still.'

worked. The brilliant civilization which has risen on his horizon is not a world above him to which he is admitted on sufferance, but his spiritual home, the bond of union being Desdemona's love. His whole nature is fulfilled—its frustrated desire for beauty, its unfathomable goodness—and as his vitality is tremendous, all his being rushes like a torrent down the newly made channel. When the shock comes that reverses the impulse, racial origins reassert themselves and he does deeds of horror. The evil that enters Shakespeare's world with Iago is stronger than in *Hamlet*, for it can transform a good man like Othello to a devil; and in the upturning of his nature from the depths foul things come to light.

The final depths open in *Lear* where the King struggles for moral and spiritual self-preservation in a world that is relapsing to nature. There was a passage in the Koran beloved of Carlyle: 'Thou hast made men having compassion on one another.' This law fails in the world of *Lear* where humanity preys on itself like monsters from the deep. Such wickedness is more terrifying than that of Iago, which was cultured and individual, for it is like a blind urge from a central store which is part of the constitution of the universe. Edmund proclaims nature to be his goddess, rejects everything but power, passion, sensuality. Goneril and Regan break the holiest ties without a pang of conscience. Can we truly say that our last impression is that good has conquered evil? Does not the sound of Lear's grief for Cordelia fill the world, and make insignificant the work of Kent, Edgar, Albany, in the good cause? To take a transcendental or other-worldly view of Cordelia's fate is to contradict the conditions of the drama. We can only surmise that as this world has a definite part to play in making a human soul, when the soul has endured the uttermost and can learn nothing more from earth, it matters little if its material tenement is shattered.

To find a personal Shakespearian clue to *Macbeth* is

equally hard, although the triumph of evil brings no happiness. In killing Duncan, Macbeth has killed his own soul; he can enjoy nothing of the position on which he has ventured all to achieve, is restless in the present, and preoccupied with the future. No human ties bind him, except to his wife, and even her death does not affect him strongly. The reconciling thing is his poet's nature, the splendour of his imagery. The man who could utter such thoughts on sleep has not long fallen from heaven.

The student of Shakespeare's impartiality and universality hardly dares advance any theory of his private relation to the great tragedies, yet there are certain haunting passages and recurring themes that do seem extra-dramatic. One of these is Lear's question, 'Is there any cause in nature that makes these hard hearts?' (III. 6). We recall the banished Duke of *As You Like It* in the forest (II. 1):

> 'Here feel we but the penalty of Adam,
> The seasons' difference; as the icy fang,
> And churlish chiding of the winter's wind,
> Which, when it bites and blows upon my body,
> Even till I shrink with cold, I smile, and say,
> This is no flattery: these are counsellors
> That feelingly persuade me what I am. . . .'

And we compare this with the bitter speech of Apemantus to the self-banished Timon (IV. 3):

> '. . . What, think'st
> That the bleak air, thy boist'rous chamberlain,
> Will put thy shirt on warm? . . .
> . . . Will the cold brook,
> Candied with ice, caudle thy morning taste,
> To cure thy o'er-night's surfeit? . . .'

When everything has been conceded to the needs of the drama, we cannot but suspect a shadow on Shakespeare's own mind. The note that persists is regret for lost happiness —fear that love and friendship and kindness may perish from the world, that man, the slave of passion, may turn earthward for ever, and continue his march indefinitely into the darkness. Yet hope never utterly dies, and widely as Shakespeare's tragic heroes differ, they have one movement of the mind in common. Part of Hamlet's tragedy was sorrow for the loss of his ideal inner world. Othello, in the tumult of his soul, does not forget the things that made earth like heaven—not only the beauty of Desdemona, not only 'the tranquil mind', but 'the plumèd troop', 'the neighing steed', 'the royal banner', 'all the pomp and circumstance of glorious war'. Lear's anger at Cordelia's seeming coldness was partly because 'he loved her most and thought to set his rest on her kind nursery'. His despair at her death is not lessened by the thought that at his age of fourscore and upward he cannot long survive. Macbeth's nature was not social even before the crime, yet he shrinks from the curses of which he is the object, and the loss in old age of 'honour, love, obedience, troops of friends'. Shakespeare's love of life survived the belt of desert that surrounds this world; he emerged unblinded by the sand-storms, with keener vision for good in man.

There is a quality in *Antony and Cleopatra* absent from the great tragedies—a mingling of pagan and spiritual, of dawn and sunset, like light over the play. The men of the Renaissance dared to be themselves for evil as well as good; we ventured to think that in the revels of Falstaff there was something not unpleasing to God. By granting man free will, as Dean Matthews has said, 'God was taking the risks of a real creation'. In Stevenson's fantasy the drug failed and Jekyll could no longer exchange with Hyde because the original drug contained something more than the compounder was aware of, and it was 'the unknown impurity that lent efficacy to the draught'. The love of Antony and Cleopatra may be pagan, yet it far transcends sense, but it certainly has no Christian tinge, for we have little faith in Antony's Elysium and the places where souls couch upon flowers, however stately the verse in which he expresses his thought. All his previous career had prepared him for his great love—battles and conquest, forced marches, and victory over hardship—but through Cleopatra he wins a happiness greater than that of fulfilled ambition. Yet his path is strewn with wrecks—the ruins of an empire, the decadence of a race, the corruption of the minds of men. In the great tragedies there was expense of spirit, but here there is waste of shame. At the moment of death he speaks like an immortal, yet he required earth for his base; and Cleopatra's grief after his death, though she too plays with visions of reunion, has the heaviness of mortality. Had Rome indeed melted in Tiber, and the arch of the Empire fallen, there would have been no Antony. The deadliest poisons have medicinal use; Cleopatra's treachery, her flight from Actium, is part of her love in this strange world. Dare we suggest that a kind of astonishment might seize the Creator at the use made of His creation by these two beings? It was the unknown impurity that lent efficacy to the draught.

Troilus and Cressida fails to subdue the reader as a whole because it contains no love or friendship. It is a chronicle of broken pledges, betrayed friendships, treachery, suspicion. The great speeches of Ulysses outstand, but they are not closely dramatic. The false dawn of the love of the two who give the play its name is a gleam over the waste, but, when quenched, the murk is deeper. Cressida, who is an artist and touches the earth but lightly, is the imaginative heart of the play. If not fire and air like Cleopatra, she has evolved to the point where matter counts for little, but her cult of the beautiful has outstripped that of the good, and the result is disaster to others if not herself. Romeo compared Juliet's eyes to two stars that had earthly business. Cressida's home is in heaven, but she also has earthly business, and fails in it like many another artist. She is constituted for free love in the spiritual world, but her vision is dulled by earthly contacts and she succumbs to free love on earth. Yet she vindicates the truth of Burke's saying, that vice loses half its evil by losing all its grossness.

As drama *Coriolanus* is compelling, but violence is done to character for the sake of plot. The true Shakespeare appears in the human relations of mother, son, husband, wife, friend, which are outside politics and greater than the laws of Rome. The reconciliation between Coriolanus and Aufidius brings us nearer to Shakespeare, because in such communion man is following his true destiny; but when, that the story should be fulfilled, Aufidius turns traitor, there is the same jar to poetic truth as with the rejection of Falstaff. There is also something strained and artificial, and therefore un-Shakespearian, in the super-contempt of Coriolanus for the plebeians.

Such contrasts are more marked in the romances, and though it would be absurd to suggest any failure of Shakespeare's dramatic power, in view of the final unravelling of the plot in *Cymbeline*, or the whole structure of the *Tempest*, we may surmise that as his career drew to a close he concentrated on what pleased him. There are crude things in *Cymbeline*, such as Iachimo's attempt to seduce Imogen; and in the *Winter's Tale*, the unfounded jealousy of Leontes; and in the *Tempest*, the forced log-carrying of Ferdinand. The reader would not have forgiven Leontes at the end had his order to burn his wife and child carried conviction. Leontes is only his true self in his friendship for Polixenes and in his repentance; Prospero, in his care for his daughter, his meditations, and his conciliation with his former enemies, not when he scolds and threatens and imposes tasks. What occupies Shakespeare is the peace and joy that human beings give to each other, but there is this difference with the comedies, that then the whole world was called in to share, but now there is selection and exclusion. In early times all men and women were potential lovers, friendships were formed in a day, love was at first sight, but now only those are accepted who have been tried in the fires of life. The spontaneous attachment between Imogen and her unknown brothers approves rather than contradicts this statement. Nor, as before, do they need the world's sympathy, but are happiest with each other—Imogen and Posthumus, Miranda and Ferdinand, Perdita and Florizel. The course of love is no longer smooth, and lovers may have to endure absence, misunderstanding, evil tongues. Perdita and Miranda surpass the women of the earlier plays because they are vicarious sufferers, and their seriousness derives from imaginative sympathy with others. They live among older people who have borne much sorrow, and they absorb this atmosphere and give it back—an atmosphere of those whose life is behind them, who are happy yet conscious of approaching death, with hope of reunion hereafter but no certainty, and therefore great kindness for the friends whom they will shortly leave. This imaginative bearing by the young of age's burden adds to their morning the beauty of twilight, to their spring the beauty of autumn. Their dwelling, in Wordsworthian phrase, is the light of setting suns.

Shakespeare's philosophy may be summed up as social-divine, because at the heart of the plays we find the joy, hope, comfort, the immortality on earth, that human beings afford each other. It is the natural atmosphere of the comedies, in the histories it has to compromise with national events, in the tragedies it engages in battles with evil that are sometimes indecisive, in the romances it is the consolation of the few who reach the lotus land. If I *Henry IV* is the greatest history it is because state affairs are subordinate to persons, while in *Henry V* state affairs prevail. Except in his fullest tragic power, when he becomes like a god knowing good and evil, Shakespeare's hand wavers when he depicts evil and treachery, as if these things were against his nature. After his tragic period he gladly forgets his terrible lesson and returns to his former innocence. Among such lapses are the King's denial of his old friend, Antonio's persecution of Shylock, the doubtful psychology of Angelo, the recantation of Aufidius, the excessive insolence of Coriolanus and the pride of

Bertram, Isabella's harshness to her brother, the belief of Posthumus in Imogen's guilt, and that of Leontes in Hermione's, the role of taskmaster assumed by Prospero. Against his dramatic intention we sympathize with Shylock and Malvolio, and, because he was more at home with love than hate, we accept the impossible conversions of the villains of *As You Like It*. The revels of Falstaff, the roguery of Autolycus, prove that a super-region of humour exists where material objects are but the playthings of mind. Because he is a fortune-hunter, Bassanio does not appear less like a true lover in our eyes. Love makes light of worldly things, and friends have all things in common. There is excess of love in *Midsummer Night's Dream*, like a river in flood that sweeps away bridges and makes impassable roads by which normal human intercourse is conducted. In the tragedies he shows by examples such as Lear, Othello, Macbeth that when man is caught up in the whirlwind of passion he is alienated from God, a destroyer of his fellow men. Yet of his major evildoers, King Claudius, Macbeth, Lady Macbeth, even Edmund, are not untouched by the mercy of God; only the names of Iago, Goneril, and Regan are blotted from the book of life.

We need not ask what were Shakespeare's intellectual beliefs, for we see his whole nature respond to the social-divine, and his genius heightened when he depicts kindly relations. You would think that when Bertram calls Diana 'a common gamester to the camp', and Angelo describes Mariana's reputation as 'dissolved in levity', they had finally placed themselves beyond the bounds of forgiveness, and, equally, when Isabella prays 'a thousand prayers' for her brother's death; but these things are mere stage devices to serve the plot, like Shakespeare's breaches of psychology; they are not reality: for when we hear the rhythmic speech of his characters, their minds come close to our own, and we know there is something truer than the material world, where we and they are one, where Falstaff is no thief and wine-bibber but our beloved friend, and so by another road we enter Paradise. The drama is not concerned with the world hereafter, yet from the mystery-silences that occur in reading Shakespeare the thought is born that the love of our fellow creatures is neither vain nor transitory, that there is something in the universe that justifies the fine frenzy of Romeo and Juliet, sympathizes with Malvolio's fallen hopes or Shylock's ill-treatment or Antony's defeat, condones Falstaff's excesses; that if we put our trust in human love we shall find our souls. Modern philosophers say that there is no such thing as love of man apart from love of God; and Shakespeare's unspoken moral is that where two or three are gathered together in love there is God in the midst. The great mystics assure us that as man needs God, so God needs man, and if God needs man it is to love him. If man is made in God's image, he is most godlike who creates most and loves most, and few can dispute the first place with Shakespeare.

V

MILTON

Milton, in his youth, was the true poet who reconciled art and life. His circumstances favoured the writing of poetry, and his poetry increased his personal distinction. Until the outbreak of the civil war he lived the ideal life of one who cultivates great natural gifts among good surroundings. He was fortunate in his home, as the son of an excellent father who believed in him, and gave him every chance to acquire knowledge, and exempted him from the need of earning money. At Cambridge his developing literary powers, impressive personality, and good looks won him an extraordinary reputation. The years that followed, in the seclusion of Horton, Buckinghamshire, were spent in reading and re-reading the Greek and Roman poets and thus consolidating the gains of his university career. His travels in France and Italy and acquaintance with some of the leading scholars in Europe were a fitting epilogue to his protracted education, and prologue to the great work forming in his mind but not to be accomplished for twenty years. This interlude of his fiery political career has been called a blessing in disguise, adding knowledge of reality to his equipment, and producing the richest fruit of his poetical rebirth—the character of Satan. If, however, we examine the inner spirit of his verse, we shall see that the finer beauty which perished when he exchanged literature for politics did not entirely reappear in the great works of his culmination, and that among the might-have-beens of literature is the *Odyssey*-like charm of his early writings never further developed.

These early poems show the perfect balance of art and life.

The *Allegro* and *Penseroso* are diffuse in the good sense of the word, and might be extended indefinitely. The subjects rise to his memory at haphazard and are written down in gold. They are the divided experience of books and country life, memories of childhood and the university, but the essential thing is the pause which follows the imprint of each image upon the reader's mind. That pause gives us Milton's spirit —serious, but pleased with life because it is the ready material of art, because it has seen his dreams fulfilled and given substance to the visions that sprang from his readings in much-loved books. It is not facile art, but the difficulties are straightforward, and on his side are youth, happiness, energy, and none of those preoccupations with material needs that hinder inspiration. The test of prosperity is a hard one, as Carlyle said of Goethe, but youth takes happiness for granted, and Milton at this period emerges from it in triumph. He was always a conscious writer, and here each stroke of beauty is consciously designed, but the animating spirit is freer, more concerned with the present, less otherworldly than in his after-writings. This earth is a very fair copy of heaven, and his impressions mingle with his thoughts on books, so that his lines are like echoes, now far off, now more near, subtly controlling one another. The following are among his most perfect and characteristic lines:

'Come; but keep thy wonted state,
With even step, and musing gait,
And looks commercing with the skies:
Thy rapt soul sitting in thine eyes:
There, held in holy passion still,
Forget thyself to marble. . . .'

As life and learning meet, the poet's mind is kindled to fire which subsides like the after-glow of sunset, and we read his meaning in the light of the stars that crowd upon each other. Milton's youthful impulse was entirely lyric, and his deeper mind in *Lycidas* overshadowed the formal subject, as in these lines, among the most fascinating in English poetry, but entirely unconcerned with the fate of Edward King:

'Rough Satyrs danced, and Fauns with cloven heel
From the glad sound would not be absent long;
And old Damoetas loved to hear our song.'

There is no more sorrow in *Lycidas* than melancholy in the *Penseroso*, but in both a grave spiritual joy because earth is like heaven, and the great minds of the past witness to this, as well as the beauty of sunlight and shadow, of green lawns and bursts of spring flowers, and the ordinary affairs of life as seen through the scholar's window.

A mind at peace with itself and unembittered by external conflict was that of Milton in his youth, because he was happy in his domestic circumstances, his genius was recognized by all who came into contact with him, and the earth was fair. The perfect result of his early poetic life was *Comus*. His genius was not dramatic, and only in the Satan of *Paradise Lost* did he draw the character of an enemy with sympathy. *Comus* is no exception, and the arguments of the Enchanter are confuted at every turn; but, unlike the previous poems, the leading idea governs throughout and adds beauty to the separate passages. This idea—the praise of chastity—throws much light on Milton's psychology of the moment. It is best expressed by the Elder Brother in such lines as these:

'Till oft converse with heavenly habitants
Begin to cast a beam on the outward shape,
The unpolluted temple of the mind,
And turns it by degrees to the soul's essence,
Till all be made immortal.'

This is pure Platonism, but also characteristic of Milton, and proves again that the mind can only learn what it knows already. No doubt it was that 'beam on the outward shape' which had won Milton at Cambridge the nickname of 'The

Lady'. But though his theme in *Comus* is abstinence and chastity, this earth is no waste space and life no empty gift. Earth is the approach to heaven, and the old truth of sacrificing life in order to regain it in a far richer form is here. The gates of the House Beautiful are closed to the self-indulgent, but a thousand unsuspected beauties visit the undimmed senses of those who live rightly. At this period Milton was less preoccupied with other-worldliness than the earthward aspect of heaven. Life is a Garden of Eden where man walks with his fellows, but not yet with God Himself. The scale is so weighted in favour of goodness that we never tremble for the Lady's safety; there is no fear that she will succumb to the temptations of the Enchanter, or that the Brothers will fail in their work of rescue. Some sympathy for frailty, lighter condemnation of those who are less than perfect would have made Milton's nature more complete and aided his dramatic power. It is needless to recall that in *Comus* he drew largely on the episode of Circe in the *Odyssey* and the sailors turned to swine. Homer tells how, when the comrades of Odysseus regained their human shape, they wept for joy, and the rest of the company wept also, in the joy of reunion, and even the enchantress was moved with compassion[1]; but it was not in Milton to add this last divine touch. If he had written the *Iliad*, would Achilles have restored the body of Hector?

The twenty years that intervened between Milton's early and final poetic activity were given to politics and embittered by blindness and domestic trouble. It is tempting to speculate on what might have been the type of the great poem that lay submerged in his mind, and conclude that it would have attained a purer beauty even than *Paradise Lost* had his life continued on its first course, had the war of pamphlets not claimed him, had he found with his wife and children the same happiness as in his father's house. Milton has been called 'unamiable' by Mark Pattison, and Dr. Johnson uses

[1] *Odyssey*, X. 399: '. . .θεὰ δ'ἐλέαιρε καὶ αὐτή'.

the word 'savageness' of his political conflicts, but Mark Pattison rightly says that one with the sensibility of a poet should have held aloof from politics, and it is equally obvious that over-sensitiveness, besides want of perception, was the cause of much of his private sorrow. He is thought to have been austere and solitary, but he was glad to converse with learned men, and in later years his company was sought by distinguished foreigners who visited England. He was touched by the kind visits of friends after he became blind, and describes their 'tender assiduities, their soothing attentions, their reverential observances'.[1] In his pamphlets on divorce the cry never ceases of wounded sensitiveness and thwarted sociality. 'In God's intention', he writes, 'a meet and happy conversation is the chiefest and the noblest end of marriage.'[2] No doubt he was inclined to dominate, but his nature would have expanded with happiness, and he might have conceded to love what he refused to opposition. Had his great work filled the years that followed *Comus*, there would have been a lesser decline from the ideal. Some readers hold that the character of Satan is compensation.

In the past, critics have often concentrated on the first two books of *Paradise Lost* and exalted the character of Satan above the softer passages. They have seen in him an idealized transcription of the poet's own experience—his undaunted courage in adversity, his unbroken confidence in the justice of the cause that was shattered beyond hope by the Restoration, his defiance to the last of his victorious enemies. All this is true, and it is equally true that only here does Milton excel in dramatic power, so that the duel between good and evil is not one-sided and prejudged. But the grandeur of the first two books and some of the later Satanic speeches must not blind us to the finer essence of the poem. *Paradise Lost* belongs neither to youth nor age but to the whole of life, and if in youth we have admired excessively the presentment of Satan, with increasing years we choose the stillness of the

[1] *The Second Defence of the People of England.* [2] *Divorce*, I. 2.

softer books. As author of one of the world's great poems, Milton should be compared with other world-poets and his unique quality defined. In the first two books he owes much to Homer, Aeschylus, Virgil, among others, and though Dryden called him a 'celestial thief'—and it is well said that a phrase belongs to him who can make best use of it—and he often equals his originals, yet he seldom surpasses them, so that we must look elsewhere for his greatest contribution to world-poetry. It may also be urged that he initiates into the mysteries of Greek and Latin literature persons unacquainted with those languages—that whereas formal translations are true only to the letter, he is true to the spirit, and re-echoes the thunders of the *Iliad* and *Prometheus Bound*. But this is a secondary virtue, and even at the height of the storm the greatest effect is produced by the still small voice. The opening lines of the poem, the remorse of Satan for his followers, the songs and discourses of the angels after Satan's departure are all unsurpassed in beauty. The following lines are an instance of what we shall discover to be the essential charm in the central books:

'. . . Angel Forms, who lay entranced
Thick as autumnal leaves that strow the brooks
In Vallombrosa, where the Etrurian shades
High over-arched embower.'

To return to the classics, the muster-roll of the angels, who afterwards became heathen idols, is taken from two scenes in Homer—the assembling of the Myrmidons, and Achilles arraying himself in the new armour—and, except in a few lines, is inferior.[1] Satan's flight across Chaos is less obviously modelled upon the struggle of Achilles with the river Scamander,[2] but does suggest comparison: and here also, by the standard of world-poetry, Homer is supreme. Likewise, Satan's defiance of the Almighty must yield in grandeur to that which the Prometheus of Aeschylus hurls

[1] *Iliad*, XVI. 155 ff.; XIX. 350 ff.

[2] *Ibid.* XXI.

back on Zeus. There is even a hint of trespass when he enters the very highest regions, for though, in describing the rout of Satan's hosts by the son of God, he has re-imagined truly certain passages of Homer, the pleasures of reminiscence fail, because the reader's mind yearns for the unapproachable splendour of the rout of the Trojans by Achilles. Virgil's Elysium[1] inspired the music and philosophy of the milder among Milton's fallen angels—and to Virgil belongs the prize. There is a lyric note in Milton, the admission of something personal, only half relevant, into his epic theme, whereas Virgil's beauty is intrinsic: as if—contrary to Plato[2] —the harmony which is of heaven had survived the shattering of the lyre made by the hands of men and continued to sound on earth. This is not to forget the pleasure of allusion, in which no poet has excelled Milton, and there is another standard than superiority or inferiority to the original. This may be more easily tested when reminiscence depends on a single word. Homer speaks of the minstrel Demodocus whom the muse had amerced (ἄμερσε) of his sight but granted him the divine gift of song.[3] Milton attributes remorse to Satan as he surveys the ranks of fallen angels—'millions of spirits for his fault *amerced* of heaven'.[4] It is not a question of order of merit, but whether the mere fact of allusion, of recalling the past, does not produce a third beauty which neither of these passages would possess independently: a question that can be raised but not answered. Allusion, however, though a high poetic office, is not the highest, and it is of this that we are in search.

It is not in the louder sounds that we find the unique

[1] *Aeneid*, VI. 637–65. Virgil no doubt derived his Elysium from Pindar's *Dirge*. Pindar wrote of a sun that shines while it is night in the human world, of crimson-flowered meadows, of the inhabitants who delight in bodily feats, and dice, and harp-playing. . . . This is paralleled by Virgil's 'ampler ether', special sun and stars, wrestling ground, music, dance, song, arms and chariots, chanting of the paean, fragrant laurel groves.

[2] *Phaedo*, 86. [3] *Odyssey*, VIII. 64. [4] *P. L.*, I. 609–10.

Miltonic quality, but in their graded decline to a centre of calm. The scenes in the Garden of Eden have been disparaged by some critics of the past as uninteresting pictures of a Puritan and his wife; but this is far from the truth. In his description of the happiness of Adam and Eve, Milton has passed beyond his subject and touched the heart of reality. The subject of the poem is the loss of happiness, and there is, therefore, an obvious pathos in the position of the two surrounded with beauty and innocence and watched by angelic guards, all of which they will shortly lose. But the final emotion is not grief for loss, nor is it romantic—where imagination has made earth so like heaven that we wake in sorrow to find it only a dream. Milton has outranged his subject, has created a state of happiness that does not pass away, and made us immortal by the music of words. Mystics say that when the mind has attained to the world of four dimensions, beyond time and space, they are conscious that all the beautiful things of the past still exist—all the Greek statues ground to powder by the barbarians, all the Egyptian temples that once dotted the valley of the Nile.[1] So we feel that though Satan triumphs, and Adam and Eve are driven from Paradise, the city endures that has been built to music. By attaining at moments to absolute beauty Milton proves that innocent happiness of man and woman in each other, under the care of God, is a timeless fact of the universe. In *Comus* earth was beautiful in proportion as man obeyed the laws of God, but God Himself was still beyond the clouds. Here His Presence is given, so that earth not only reflects the glory of heaven but is part of it. We may brood over a passage like this:

> 'On which the sun more glad impressed his beams
> Than in fair evening cloud, or humid bow
> When God hath showered the earth; so lovely seemed
> That landskip.'[2]

[1] See Conway of Alington, *A Pilgrim in Quest of the Divine.*

[2] IV. 150.

Or this:

'Not distant far from thence a murmuring sound
Of waters issued from a cave, and spread
Into a liquid plain; then stood unmoved,
Pure as the expanse of Heaven.'[1]

Or this single line:

'Grace was in all her steps, heaven in her eye.'[2]

As the music of the words subsides, we feel the stillness that is the centre of the poem. *Paradise Lost* is for all our years, and in youth we were held captive by lines like these, from one of Satan's earliest speeches:

'Seest thou yon dreary plain, forlorn and wild,
The seat of desolation, void of light,
Save what the glimmering of these livid flames
Casts pale and dreadful?'[3]

But with age we transfer our love to the following, with the mystic hush that surrounds it:

'Both Heaven and Earth, wherein the just shall dwell'.[4]

And yet, when the book is closed and the reader's mind occupied only with memories, the island of peace has sunk slightly below the verge. The might of Satan outstands, the caves of Hell, the battles on the plains of Heaven, the victory of the Serpent. We need not retract our former verdict that in the Garden of Eden Milton attained reality, but the faith which we receive from him is fitful—we believe, but we need help for our unbelief. There remained one earthly spot in Milton's composition never etherealized into poetry. He could not forgive his enemies, the past was with him, he had lost faith in life and failed to achieve philosophic calm. The war between good and evil continued in his mind and cast its glare upon his page. Satan has sinned beyond forgiveness, and even if he did repent, the God he has offended is Justice,

[1] IV. 453. [2] VIII. 488. [3] I. 180–3. [4] XI. 901.

not Mercy, and would turn away. In *Comus* the transmutation was complete, because it was that of his happy academic youth, but in *Paradise Lost* there was more to be transmuted, and the facts of life had wounded his soul. The impression from *Paradise Lost* is that evil has triumphed—as it is not from *Othello* and *Lear*, despite the sacrifice of the innocent. Man in Eden is too dependent on God and cannot stand alone. Heaven does more than its rightful share, and when the fruit is tasted and the Guardian Angels forsake Paradise, the charm vanishes at a breath and leaves human nature naked and ashamed.

Milton was a learned and allusive poet, but in *Paradise Lost* he went beyond all acquired knowledge and spoke the soul's universal language. The summit of *Paradise Regained* may be compared with Sinai, where he speaks with God and receives the tablets of stone on which is written the moral law. The poem is rather a meditation, for the interest of the outer events is not compelling. The scales are as heavily weighted against Satan as they were against Comus or Adam and Eve. We never doubt the issue, and Milton's lack of sympathy for the outcast makes the victory too easily won to awake satisfaction. This, however, applies to the externals and to the working of his conscious mind, but his unconscious mind has contributed a quality less beautiful than in *Paradise Lost* but full of interest. It comes to us in the pauses and rhythms of the blank verse, in the echoes that prolong themselves in our minds after the conclusion of a period. The following will serve as an instance:

> 'Shall I seek glory, then, as vain men seek,
> Oft not deserved? I seek not mine, but His
> Who sent me, and thereby witness whence I am.'[1]

The state of Milton's life is the key to the mystery of *Paradise Regained*—'blind, old, and lonely', as Shelley said, disappointed in his human relations, unable to forgive, but

[1] III. 105–7.

with one precious possession: he can at times forget the raging past and the evil tongues of men, in the joy of solitary communion with God and meditation on the sacredness of the moral law. This final peace distilled through his pages may separate rather than unite him with the active world, but it is pure and beautiful. In his last years Milton turned to Hebrew writers rather than Greek and Latin, and this provides a secondary interest. When he touches a classical theme it is ostensibly to show the vanity of all knowledge compared with knowledge of God, but his earlier loves will not be easily dismissed. They have helped to build his mind, and they reassert their charm at the moment of farewell—like the vintage that bears witness by stored sunlight to summer days that have waned for ever over fair prospects. When he writes,

> 'See there the olive-grove of Academe
> Plato's retirement . . .'[1]

we feel no retrospective longing or sentimental regret, but the expression of a mind that has topped the ladder of learning and looks upward to the heavenly signs.

Milton's detractors have found in *Samson* final proof of his vindictiveness, his imaginative delight in the wholesale destruction of his enemies. Certainly there is the same lack of dramatic power that made it impossible for the reader to sympathize with Comus or the Satan of *Paradise Regained.* The outer events and the final catastrophe do not equal the grandeur of *Paradise Lost*, and the unrhymed, short-lined choruses are not a welcome new element. They are prosaic, and point to a failing command over verse rather than the appearance of any new power; though there are exceptions where something is captured of the rhythm of the Hebrew prophets, in such lines as 'Go and the Holy One of Israel be thy guide . . .', or the famous, 'But he, though blind of sight . . .' *Samson*, however, does possess a quality present in

[1] IV. 244–5.

no other of Milton's poems, and it is contained in the opening soliloquy. The utter loneliness of a defeated human soul is what strikes us first, but as we read and meditate we discover that to this soul, defeated yet repentant, God is present; and it has been well said that true repentance is better assurance of forgiveness than the testimony of an angel.

The apologists have selected the concluding words of *Samson*, 'Calm of mind, all passion spent', as proof of that ultimate reconciliation which the foregoing pages have denied. But if there is a calm, the cause is rather the numbness and exhaustion that follow a catastrophe than increase of spiritual knowledge. Like Virgil, Milton did not attain to the steady vision of an earthly-heavenly kingdom. In the relative perfection of his early poems, earth was made like to heaven because both soul and intellect were free to expand in earth's pleasant places. In *Paradise Lost* we glimpse the perfect union, because the beloved hours—as Theocritus called them—that bring gifts to all mortals have restored to him the gift of art; yet the reader who has released the angel and would search out the truth cannot escape a doubt whether the blessing is authentic. In the last phase the clouds re-gather, and only a Being from beyond can vanquish evil; and the only kind of happiness that survives is the true repentance of a captive in chains. It is sad but true that he remained a fighter to the last, that his armour of combativeness is not pierced nor his heart touched. The last word, therefore, despite his greatness is 'frustration'. The man who paid this tribute to the power of music,

> 'Dissolve me into ecstasies,
> And bring all Heaven before mine eyes',[1]

was among the most sensitive which the human race has produced, and cannot have lacked that consideration for others which is called 'the good breeding of the mind'. Yet he censures as 'arrogant' the young man who replied to our

[1] *Penseroso.*

Lord that all his life he had kept the commandments.[1] Surely he had forgotten the words of St. Mark, 'Then Jesus beholding him loved him'.

The emotions due to the poet from the reader are admiration, awe, and love, but with Milton it is hard to concede the last. The poet's way is from earth to heaven, but Milton, when he started upon his second poetical life, after his disillusion with the world, sought first the Kingdom of God, and all things else were not added to him, because the cause of his choice was disappointment, and had circumstances been other, life might have possessed him. In his early poems, especially *Comus*, the love of earthly beauty for its own sake does break through his theology, but not in the later, and the want excludes him from the company of the very highest—from Homer and Shakespeare. We recognize the central calm of *Paradise Lost*—the vision of perfect love—but we need to make constant returns to it, and re-confirm ourselves in its truth, lest we forget. What never fails is the Miltonic rhythm, from the moment of initiation, when we first called upon this mighty spirit to haunt us through the years: the grand harmonies of the long verse paragraphs like the distant sea, sounding every scale, from the soft lapping of the moonlit surf to the thunder of the billows that shake the earth far inland, as the chariot of the Son of God shook Heaven's basis.

[1] *Divorce*, II. 9.

VI

WORDSWORTH

It is difficult to believe that Wordsworth was decried and held up to ridicule for a large part of his life—although Coleridge from the first recognized his work as that of a great and original genius, and hailed him as the finest poet of the age. Since the turning of the tide, a splendid body of appreciative criticism has gathered round him. The great critics of the last half of the nineteenth century—Arnold, Morley, Myers, Pater, Stephen—were devoted Wordsworthians, and the tradition has been well preserved in the present century by Bradley, Garrod, Legouis, and others, culminating in the great work of Professor de Selincourt. The late-coming critic, abashed by the presence of so many masters, might shirk the issue and make of an essay on Wordsworth a summary of previous criticism and reconciliation of different viewpoints, but the truth always remains that the greatest subjects are inexhaustible, and even the newest critic, who opens his mind without prejudice to the light and takes note of those parts of it which kindle in response, may contribute something. With this purpose in mind, and the parallel purpose of experiencing in Wordsworth that which is beyond time and space, it will be necessary neither to forget the verdicts of the great commentators nor to consider that any one of them has spoken the final word.

Wordsworth himself likened the *Prelude* and *Excursion* to the ante-chapel and body of a Gothic church, and his minor poems to its little cells, oratories, and sepulchral recesses; and Myers, taking up the comparison, said that posterity had chosen to worship in the separate shrines rather than the main edifice. This opinion obtained for years, until, as if by the silent pressure of a great natural force, the long poems conquered the minds of readers: much as the huge peak, ever growing in stature, towered up between the boy Wordsworth and the stars, on that memorable summer evening when he stealthily embarked in a strange boat and rowed towards a distant point. And as the peak seemed to stride after him with purpose of its own, so do these poems follow us and haunt us like the huge and mighty forms that moved slowly through his mind for many days after the experience. Wordsworth's lack, compared with the great poets—with effect not entirely in his disfavour—was the persuasive, ornamental beauty of verse. It has been said that he disobeyed his own laws of poetic diction with the best result for himself, that had he observed them to the letter he would have failed. But the entire effect of his work remains absolutely simple. The eye that surveys the Wordsworthian field is not distracted from its examination of the whole by any exceptionally bright blossom. The old test that poetry is only poetry if its content cannot be equally well expressed in prose still holds, and it must be admitted that Wordsworth often uses words like a prose writer; but, once more, there is gain as well as loss. We say that a true poem means itself—that its matter cannot be separated from its form and sound. Few of Wordsworth's shorter poems equal, and none surpass, *Tintern Abbey*, yet it is possible to separate from its structure a deeply interesting meaning even if conveyed in prose.

It has lately been remarked that the *Excursion* contains the raw material of several good novels, and this implies that it might have been as well or even better written in prose. The total effect of his two great poems, however, is poetic in the highest sense, and this is the greatest praise that can be awarded to any work of art. Thoughts of mountains always rise to the mind when dwelling with Wordsworth, and so one may say that a mountain appears tumbled and broken when seen close at hand, but the same mountain from a distance wears a robe of purple—like the Skiddaw of his own country. Wordsworth's poetry is the expression of a great experience that has preceded its birth. It is anti-lyric in the sense that a lyric is incomplete in the maker's mind until it is written—until the words that flash upon him in the crisis of composition have revealed a further meaning. One way of realizing Wordsworth's originality is to search for likenesses to other poets. It was a fertile comparison by Matthew Arnold of Keats with Shakespeare, throwing much light on both. The critic must set his mind to a long task of discovery to find a parallel with Wordsworth. Hesiod deals with the common things of life, and so does Crabbe, but they lack Wordsworth's idealism and his power to transfigure. William Langland has his moral fervour but not his beauty. I can think of but one passage of verse that has the Wordsworthian ring; it is spoken by the Duke, who is among Shakespeare's most attractive characters, at the conclusion of *Measure for Measure*, and though it consists of simple statements and directions, every word strikes home, because the Duke has become the keeper of the whole experience of every actor in the drama, and he utters it forth:

'She, Claudio, that you wrong'd, look you restore.
Joy to you, Mariana! love her, Angelo:
I have confessed her and I know her virtue.
Thanks, good friend Escalus, for thy much goodness:
There's more behind that is more gratulate.
Thanks, provost, for thy care and secrecy;
We shall employ thee in a worthier place.
Forgive him, Angelo, that brought you home
The head of Ragozine for Claudio's:
The offence pardons itself.'

Not only is it difficult to compare Wordsworth with other poets, but it is equally difficult to realize that he was a great reader. We rather resent any intervening experience between nature and his mind. Many poets—notably Virgil and

Milton—charm by their allusiveness, but we cannot say this of Wordsworth. From the time of Macrobius in the fourth century A.D., with his parallel passages of Homer and Virgil, critics have delighted in these recognitions, but there is a feeling of strain, almost of affectation—if one dare use the word —when Wordsworth, in the *Prelude*,[1] recalls one of Horace's finest odes[2]:

> 'Smooth life had flock and shepherd in old time,
> Long springs and tepid winters, on the banks
> Of delicate Galesus. . . .'

How different is the effect of Milton's Horatian allusions in the *Allegro* and *Penseroso*!

> 'Haste thee, Nymph, and bring with thee
> Jest, and youthful Jollity. . . .'
>
> . . . .
>
> 'Come, pensive Nun, devout and pure,
> Sober, steadfast, and demure,
> All in a robe of darkest grain,
> Flowing with majestic train,
> And sable stole of cypress lawn
> Over thy decent shoulders drawn.'[3]

Here there is the pleasure of recognition, and the heightened admiration for the original and its transplanted and remoulded new version. Those lines of Wordsworth's on Newton and Spenser, since they are among his most famous, seem to contradict the theory that he most excels when he has forgotten the presence of man and is alone with nature[4]:

> '. . . I could behold
> The ante chapel where the statue stood
> Of Newton with his prism and silent face,
> The marble index of a mind for ever
> Voyaging through strange seas of thought alone.'
>
> . . . .

[1] VIII. 173–5. [2] II. 6. [3] Cf. Horace, *Odes*, I. 2.
[4] *Prelude*, III. 59–63, 280–1.

'Sweet Spenser moving through his clouded heaven
With the moon's beauty and the moon's soft pace.'

In the first there is beauty and strangeness, in the second beauty predominates, and yet the subjects of both are absorbed in nature. We do not think of the discoverer of the law of gravitation, or the poet of the *Faerie Queene*, but of that

'... all pervading Spirit upon whom
Our dark foundations rest....'[1]

We think of vast distances and lonely regions where man is not; of the stars in their inevitable courses, unconscious of human affairs. Again, how different is it with Milton when he calls upon

'Blind Thamyris and blind Maeonides,
And Tiresias and Phineus, prophets old'.[2]

Acquaintance with the story of Wordsworth's life would seem to confirm the theory that he is most himself when alone with nature. Professor Harper writes that up to a certain point he was guided by hope, and later driven by fear; and the two halves of his life are incongruous. He became a nervous Tory, opposing the Reform Bill and every other project for improvement; he lived in fear of a world-catastrophe, and attributed his own premature decline to anxiety about the fate of his country. We are accustomed to think of him as a hardy mountaineer who spent his life in the open air, and—on the intellectual side—as sublimely self-confident; yet Coleridge remarked that he suffered much from hypochondria, and at times he doubted his own poetic power. The strain of composition and the physical act of writing exhausted him, and he needed the constant stimulus of his sister Dorothy's encouragement. He did not yield without a struggle, but disputed every inch of the ground against the advancing shadow of despondency, bravely determining to

1 *Excursion*, IV. 969–70. 2 *P. L.*, III. 35–6.

be happy, regarding happiness as the equivalent to the soul of health to the body, without which man does not live in harmony with the universe. If he was finally worsted in the struggle, the reason is a lesser incongruity between the two halves of his life than Professor Harper thinks.

Let us consider some of the greatest lines in his two long poems, and attempt to deduce the whole Wordsworth from them, not one or other portion of his being:

> 'The ghostly language of the ancient earth'[1]
>
> . . . .
>
> 'The froward chaos of futurity'[2]
>
> . . . .
>
> 'That he broke Faith with them whom he had laid
> In earth's dark chambers with a Christian's hope'[3]
>
> . . . .
>
> 'Who from the anarchy of dreaming sleep,
> Or from its death-like void . . .'[4]
>
> . . . .
>
> 'The trepidations of mortality'[5]
>
> . . . .
>
> 'Far nearer in the habit of her soul
> To that still region whither all are bound'[6]
>
> . . . .
>
> 'The gleams of his slow-varying countenance'[7]

There is one emotion common to all these lines, and it is awe. He himself tells us how, as a child, he was conscious of the mysterious and unseen: when he visited the snares by night and heard low breathings and ghostly steps; when, hanging upon the crag above the raven's nest, he heard a strange note in the loud, dry wind; above all, when he unloosed the boat and was surprised by the shadow of the huge peak; and also when, separated from his comrade, he reached the spot in a deep valley where a murderer had been hanged, and was

[1] *Prelude*, I. 309. [2] *Ibid.* V. 349. [3] *Excursion*, II. 247–8.
[4] *Ibid.* IV. 87–8. [5] *Ibid.* IV. 423. [6] *Ibid.* VII. 228–9.
[7] *Ibid.* VII. 461.

appalled by the visionary dreariness of the moorland waste, the naked pool, the beacon, intensified by the wind against which he battled. Many more instances might be selected, but these are enough to show that fear and awe were prominent in the child's mind. When we read his reflections on the French Revolution we are surprised that one with a poet's sensitiveness was not more shocked by the September massacres and the Terror, till we know from his dreams that the horror had lodged in his subconscious mind. By day he shared the hope and intoxication that was in the air, but at night

'. . . the hour of sleep
To me came rarely charged with natural gifts,
Such ghastly visions had I of despair
And tyranny, and implements of death;
And innocent victims sinking under fear.'[1]

Awe is the deepest religious emotion, fear is spiritual failure, and yet they are related. If we study the lines quoted from his poems and these adventures of his childhood, we may infer that though awe possessed his soul, fear was not far in the background. It was the passage of awe into fear that defeated him in later life. We may regret the decline, but he himself never diverged from the path of a poet's ideal, as he conceived it; and we must give thanks that we can extract from the record of his childhood a message of hope, a universal truth. It is ill to jest, as some have done, at the orthodox views of his old age, and compare them with his revolutionary fervour: the cause was the insistent pressure of life upon the material habitation of the soul. His sister broke down in later years from the effects of excessive mountain walking, and with him we must count besides 'the tension of solitary thought'.[2] There are still persons who class nervous sufferers with Molière's imaginary sick man, despite the warning of a great doctor that nerves are the cause of more suffering than cancer. Carlyle was not over-tolerant, yet he

[1] *Prelude*, X. 400–4. [2] Legouis, p. 469.

admitted as reality 'the gloom of broken nerves' in the subject of one of his historical portraits. The fate of the best loved of the gods is known, and perhaps it is unjust to quote against Wordsworth his own rendering:

> '. . . the good die first,
> And they whose hearts are dry as summer dust
> Burn to the socket.'[1]

If Wordsworth was most himself when alone with nature —and many of his poems refer to solitude—his was no unsocial nature. We need constantly to remind ourselves that the early, not the late, Wordsworth was the real man. To his schooldays at Hawkshead, the summit of his spiritual life, we shall recur, but meanwhile let us note that at Cambridge his heart 'was social, and loved idleness and joy'. Travelling through France, he mixed with the villagers and shared their rapture at the thought of the better times promised by the Revolution. There may be some truth in Professor Harper's unfavourable comparison of his correspondence with that of Charles Lamb: that whereas Lamb always found something to like in the letter he was answering, there always seemed something to displease Wordsworth; but here again he refers to later years, and it does not appear in his poetry. That he can be didactic, yet not offend, is proof of his wide humanity. Among the greatest of his characters are Beaupuy in the *Prelude* and the Wanderer in the *Excursion*. They have shunned the gold and gems of the world, as Landor would say, to point an index needle at the pole of truth. The Wanderer was set in the right way from the beginning, but Beaupuy, handsome, passionate, high-born, had lived the same worldly life as his brother officers until roused by the Revolution to the service of man. With him Wordsworth only touches upon faults for the sake of their sublimation, telling how his former passion and gallantry for women had turned to courtesy for the mean, obscure, and homely; his

[1] *Excursion*, I. 500–2.

vanity to fondness and radiant joy. The Solitary of the *Excursion* is never quite admitted as an equal, and it is nature that does the larger half in subduing to friendship the former Jacobite and Hanoverian protagonists—gracious as is the picture of their 'courtly figures' seated upon the stump of yew.[1] There can even be heard a mild touch of rebuke in the beautiful description of the clergyman who, disappointed of patronage, had chosen to pass his life in the secluded chapelry among the mountains, and, though reconciled to his lot, still loved the sound of titled names and memory of banquets with high-born friends.[2]

Beaupuy is the sole instance of a cultivated man of the world winning his entire sympathy, and Beaupuy was the friend of his youth. Otherwise his love is poured forth on the humbly placed, extending to the blind, the deaf, even the mentally deficient, because the stilling of the conscious mind opens a way of communication with the heart of the universe. A darker shade of mystery settles upon the landscape in the mind's eye when he writes of the deaf man:

> 'And this deep mountain-valley was to him
> Soundless, with all its streams.'[3]

It is hard to think that he once became a disciple of Godwin, whose philosophy is the antipodes of his own. According to Godwin, every man is a new product, without tradition, without innate ideas, entering the world with a mind like a blank sheet of paper on which education may write as it pleases, and thus evolve perfect man and a perfect society. We can best describe Wordsworth's acceptance of these principles as a brief illness, for all his work is based upon the thought of man's soul as the product of centuries of interaction with nature. The larger part played by nature in the evolution of the soul is the core of his teaching.

His pictures of humble persons move us in proportion to

[1] *Excursion*, VI. 492–3. [2] *Ibid.* VII. 216–8.
[3] *Ibid.* VII. 404–5.

the distance which they keep within the boundary that separates natural from artificial man. With Beaupuy there was the barrier of race and language, which does play a part in eliminating the prosaic details of life. In his own experience there was surely no period more fruitful than the schooldays at Hawkshead. The hours of study were not excessive, and he was free of the good dame's cottage where he lodged, to take long early walks alone or with a friend, as he pleased, or re-enter by the latch after dusk. He was then separated from his family, but it does not appear that he suffered from homesickness or even regretted the absence of his kinsfolk. Professor Legouis remarks that Hawkshead was probably not free from the brutality which, unfortunately, is present in most English schools, and yet he does not mention it. The stories of human lives can hardly show us one more in harmony with the universe than was Wordsworth in these days. Mind and body, inner and outer life, health, exercise, books, companionship, solitude—all contributed to make him a sharer of the great secret. It is our business to gather up what we can of his experience.

Leslie Stephen remarked that Wordsworth ignored the dark side of nature revealed by the struggle for existence of animals and plants. Morley contrasted his Cumbrian dalesmen with the peasants of the French painter Millet, broken by a life of toil, straightening their loins with difficulty, and drawing gasping breath. These are truths, but since nature has evolved mind as her final aim, the higher truth is that of Wordsworth who shows the peace the mind can achieve by following nature. Arnold's impression, that in his greatest moments nature took the pen from Wordsworth, is that of the universe becoming self-conscious and passing into mind. Like the true Wordsworthian, Arnold derived pleasure from the poet's least interesting verse; and, as nothing comes amiss to the scientific worker, so any thoughts that filter through a mind so near nature as Wordsworth's are of value. When he excels we feel contact with spirit free from intellect more than with poets like Spenser, Milton, Shelley, Keats, despite the clouds of glory that attend them—more than with any English poet except Shakespeare. A modern theologian explains the Fall as man's repudiation of that fellowship with God for which he was created.[1] Wordsworth attained fellowship through nature, and he points out how we can all attain it, and draws a picture of the two states of man that result from acceptance or denial—the peaceful dwellers with nature, and the sophisticated crowds that fill the towns. His shock at the wrong course taken by the world after the French Revolution is an important biographical fact. We must never forget the beginning of the divine communication—the mighty forms that moved through his mind by day and troubled his dreams by night. What hushed the controversy between Jacobite and Hanoverian and made them friends was the still beauty of the scene that was the background of their arguments insensibly operating upon them. To the blind and deaf is vouchsafed a Presence denied to those who throng Courts and drawing-rooms where the man of meanest soul thrives the most. The last fear of those who look beyond humanity for happiness—loneliness of soul—is lifted in the presence of Wordsworth. Few minds that have been self-revealed are more attractive than his in early manhood.

Wordsworth was the poet of a local habitation, of a special corner of England, yet he is among the most transcendental. Reality is here attained, the heavenly Salem exists on English soil. Some persons do not wait for bodily death to put on immortality, and this experience stimulates rather than diminishes their joy in earthly life. A hint of this is borne to us as we attempt to follow in Wordsworth's steps, and the words of Isaiah become doubly true: 'How beautiful upon the mountains are the feet of him that bringeth good tidings!'

[1] J. S. Whale, *Christian Doctrine* (1941), p. 52.

INDEX

INDEX